Landscaping with Wildflowers & Native Plants

Created and designed by the
editorial staff of ORTHO BOOKS
Photographer: Michael McKinley
Writer: William H. W. Wilson

Photographer: Michael McKinley

Illustrator: Ron Hildebrand

Ortho Books

Publisher
Robert L. Iacopi

Editorial Director
Min S. Yee

Managing Editors
Anne Coolman
Michael D. Smith

Production Manager
Ernie S. Tasaki

Senior Editor
Sally W. Smith

Editors
Jim Beley
Susan Lammers
Deni Stein

Design Coordinator
Darcie S. Furlan

System Managers
Mark Zielinski
Christopher Banks

Photographic Director
Alan Copeland

Photographers
Laurie A. Black
Richard A. Christman
Michael D. McKinley

Production Editors
Linda Bouchard
Alice Mace
Kate O'Keeffe

Asst. System Manager
William F. Yusavage

Photo Editors
Anne Dickson-Pederson
Pam Peirce

Production Assistant
Don Mosley

National Sales Manager
Garry P. Wellman

Sales Assistant
Susan B. Boyle

Operations Director
William T. Pletcher

Operations Assistant
Gail L. Davis

Administrative Assistant
Georgiann Wright

Address all inquiries to
Ortho Books
Chevron Chemical Company
Consumer Products Division
Box 5047
San Ramon, CA 94583

Chevron Chemical Company
6001 Bollinger Canyon Road, San Ramon, CA 94583

ACKNOWLEDGMENTS

Consultants:
We wish to thank the following
people for contributing
information and for checking
the manuscript for accuracy:
John Baumgardt, Cassville, MO
Joe Brown, Mid-Atlantic
Wildflowers, Glouster Point,
VA
Panayoti Callas, Denver Botanic
Gardens, Denver, CO
Joseph A. Casuo, Landscape
Architect, Jacksonville, FL
Paul Cummings, The Tree Gallery,
Boynton Beach, FL
Edgar Dennison, St. Louis, MO
Bill Farthington, Winter Park, FL
Joyce Gann, Tropical Greenery,
Goulds, FL
Lester Hawkins, Western Hills
Nursery, Occidental, CA
Richard Hildreth, State Arboretum
of Utah, Salt Lake City, UT
David Longland, Garden-in-the-
Woods, Framingham, MA
F. M. Mooberry, The Brandywine
Conservancy, Chadds Ford,
PA
Rolf Nelson, Lilypons Water
Gardens, Brookshire, TX
Lorrie Otto, Riveridge Nature
Center, Milwaukee, WS
Harry Phillips, University of North
Carolina Botanic Garden,
Chapell Hill, NC
Judith Phillips, Bernardo Beach
Native Plant Farm, Veguita,
NM
Joyce Powers, Prairie Ridge
Nursery, Mt. Horeb, WI
Warren G. Roberts, University
Arboretum, University of
California, Davis, CA
Susan Roth, The Plant Photo
Library, Centerport, NY
Mary Sanger, Texas Department
of Agriculture, Austin, TX
Benny Simpson, Texas Agricultural
Experiment Station, Dallas,
TX

Norman Singer, American Rock
Garden Society, South
Sandisfield, MA
Dee Slinkard, Sanibel-Captiva
Conservation Foundation,
Sanibel, FL
Dr. Geoffrey Stanford, Greenhills
Center and Experimental
Station, Dallas, TX
Thomas Stille, Stille and
Associates, Reno, NV
Donald Vorpahl, Hilbert, WI
Gayle Weinstein, Denver Botanic
Gardens, Denver, CO
Margaret Williams, Northern
Nevada Native Plant Society,
Reno, NV
In addition to the above, the
author wishes to thank the
many nurseries, growers, and
native plant societies who
gave so generously of their
time and expertise.

Photo acknowledgments:
(Names of photographers,
locations, and designers are
followed by the page
numbers on which their work
appears. R = right, L = left,
T = top, B = bottom)
Additional photography: Front and
back cover photography by
Michael McKinley; Laurie
Black: 72; Walter Chandoha:
27, 55, 84; Clyde Childress:
55R, 88R; Richard Christman:
44B; Josephine Coatsworth:
28; W. Perry Conway: 23T;
Derek Fell: 53, 77; Pamela
Harper: 57L; Grant Heilman
Photography: 16, 17, 20T, 68;
Alan Klehr: 22; Michael
Landis: 33B; Ivan Massar: 5;
The Plant Library/Susan Roth:
4; David Wasserman: 9T, 10;
Will Wilson: 13; Gary R. Zahm:
66R
Garden locations: *Millstream,*
Falls Village, CT: Title Page,
89; Sonoran Desert Museum,
Tucson, AZ: 8B; The Nature

Preserve at Whitnell Park,
Hales Corner, WI: 19, 65L;
Sea Ranch, CA: 23B, 82;
Garden-in-the-Woods,
Framingham, MA: 24, 25, 34;
Panfield Nurseries, Long
Island, NY: 30; Rosedown
Gardens, Bellevue, WA: 35;
Santa Ana Botanical
Gardens, Santa Ana, CA: 72;
Pajaro Dunes, Watsonville,
CA: 82, 83; Magnolia
Gardens, Charleston, SC: 86
Garden Designers: David Benner,
New Hope, PA: 9T, 26, 51;
Frank Cabot, Cold Spring,
NY: 9B; Lawrence Halperin,
Sea Ranch: 23B; James
David, Austin, TX: 29, 49; Tom
Patterson, Panfield Nurseries,
Huntington, NY: 30;
Christopher C. Fredricks, New
Orleans, LA: 33T; Oehme,
Van Sweden and Associates,
Washington D.C.: 31; Michael
McKinley, Bolinas, CA: 32T,
32B; Lindsay Smith,
Birmingham, AL: 36; Patrick
Morgan, La Malbaie, Quebec,
Canada: 58; Ted Kipping, San
Francisco, CA: 70; Steve
Martino, Phoenix, AZ: 73;
Craig Lindquist, Carefree, AZ:
75; Phil Johnson, Lafayette,
CA: 75; Andropogon
Association, Philadelphia, PA:
92

Special thanks to: Frank Cabot,
Rick Clinebell, Gene Cisyk,
James David, Katherine Hull,
Margo Parrot
Andropogon Associates,
Philadelphia, PA
Jerry Flemming of California Native
Plants Society, Berkeley, CA
Garden-in-the-Woods,
Framingham, MA
Ron Lutsko, L.A., Lafayette, CA

Front cover:
The "alpine lawn" of
Millstream, the garden of Mr.
and Mrs. H. Lincoln Foster,
Falls Village, Connecticut

Back cover:
Top left: Birmingham, Alabama. A
southeastern woodland
garden in April with wild blue
phlox, flowering dogwood,
and American columbine.
Top right: Phoenix, Arizona. A
Sonoran desert garden with
organ pipe, giant saguaro,
beavertail cactus, yellow
bitterbrush, and yucca.

Bottom left: Quebec, Canada. An
open meadow in a northern
coniferous region with orange
and yellow hawkweed and oxeye daisy.
Bottom right: Santa Cruz,
California. Beach plantings of
dune grass and Indian
paintbrush, with exotic ice
plants as additional sand
stabilizers.

Title page:
Some of the alpine flowers shown
on the front cover. On the
right are nodding Pasque-
flowers (*Anemone pulsatilla*),
on the left a vetch (*Lathyrus
verona*).

Landscaping with Wildflowers & Native Plants

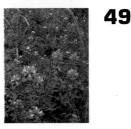

Native plants and the natural landscape

An appreciation of our native landscape leads many of us to want to bring it into our gardens. Many gardeners have done this, some with great beauty and grace.

About one hundred years ago, Henry David Thoreau wrote eloquently of the native landscape of this continent. Living on the shores of Walden Pond in eastern Massachusetts, he came to know the forest, trees, and herbs in all their seasonal moods. He watched the white pine glow in spring sunlight, trilliums and violets bloom on the forest floor, and the red maples grow brilliant with autumn. In his writings he celebrated the beauty of native plants and the natural landscape.

Other voices have spoken of the rich splendor of American native plants. Jens Jensen, landscape designer from the northern Midwest, strove in his work to recreate the "tapestry of living colors" beheld by early pioneers in the region. He loved the native dogwoods, crabapples, and hawthorns of the Midwest, and included in his designs for public parks and private estates many natural woodland landscapes, meadows, and even a meandering prairie river created within a city park.

Botanists and plant collectors have long seen great value in American native plants. Plant explorers, such as David Douglas in the Pacific Northwest, collected and sent back to Europe seed and specimens of many native American species, which were enthusiastically welcomed into European horticulture.

Bright maples beckon us into the golden world of an American autumn woodland.

Two fishermen enjoy the peaceful beauty of Walden Pond, which most of us know only through the words of Thoreau.

Despite this enthusiasm, the native plants of North America have rarely been popular in American gardens. The early ornamental gardens of Williamsburg and other colonial settlements favored the clipped yew hedges and tidy flowerbeds of Europe to the "wild and untamed" trees and flowers of nearby forests. Later American gardens were less formal, but still usually centered around the European "green sward" of lawn, and imported shrubs. As the era of worldwide plant exploration blossomed in the late 1800s, the exotic trees and shrubs of the far corners of the earth became the featured attractions of American gardens, most often combined with brilliant sweeps of hybridized bedding flowers.

In recent years, this has begun to change. The exotic favorites of years past are now sharing garden space with our own native plants—the species of North American forests, prairies, chaparral, and desert. Many people are now planting gardens that feature the native plants of their region in attractive ornamental beds, as specimen plants, and in recreated natural environments.

This book will introduce you to the native plants of North America. Separate chapters describe how these plants grow together in nature, how to design a garden with native plants, how to propagate and grow your own plants from seed and cuttings, and how to establish and maintain a native plant garden. Whatever your interest in native plants, this book will help you use them to create a beautiful garden.

Defining terms

Every plant is a native plant somewhere in the world. When grown in another area, it is usually called an *exotic* plant, to distinguish it from the native plants of that region. Scots pine, for example, a native forest tree in northern Europe and Asia, is also grown as an exotic plant in the gardens of eastern North America. The coast redwood, native to California, is grown as an exotic plant in gardens all over the world.

Another term we'll use frequently in this book is *natural landscaping*, which is the arrangement of native plants in a garden in a way similar to their arrangement in nature. Natural landscaping can mean grouping together in a garden area several native species that typically grow together in nature, sowing a meadow of the native wildflowers and grasses of your region, or adding native shrubs and ferns to open areas in an existing woodland. On a grander scale, it can mean landscaping large areas with the native species of your region, first studying nearby natural areas carefully, and then recreating as nearly as possible the soil, landforms, moisture conditions, and plant arrangements of the natural environment in your created landscape.

The pleasures of native plant gardening

Landscaping with native plants offers many unique gardening pleasures. Learning about native plants is a way of discovering many new plants for your garden, each with its unique beauties of flower, texture, branching pattern, and plant form, and many with intriguing ways of adapting to the specific growing conditions found in your region. You can use these plants in many attractive combinations with other native species, or with exotic shrubs, trees, and flowers.

The native plants of your region can also put you in touch with its history. In most parts of the country,

This "Sierra" stream runs past an urban San Francisco area home. The rocks and the red twigs of Cornus stolonifera, *still bare in early spring, complete the illusion.*

the natural environment of vegetation, landform, and wildlife has been so completely altered or destroyed that we can get few glimpses of the land as it was even a century ago. In your garden, by recreating the now-vanished prairie, woodland, or forest which once clothed your region, you can rediscover the past, and find a "sense of place"—an understanding and a tie to the land where you live. You can envision the land as Indians and pioneers must have known it, learn the plants they valued for food and beauty, and understand more of the natural character of your region.

A native plant garden can provide an escape from our modern world. Your garden can be a relaxing, retreat from the landscape of straight lines,

square corners, and unattractive streetscapes all around us. Gardens have always had the power to soothe and resuscitate the spirit; the soft forms, flowing curved lines, and bright seasonal flowers of a natural landscape can provide an especially welcome haven.

Native plants open your garden to other types of wildlife: birds, insects, deer, and small animals. You can choose combinations of native shrubs that will provide year-round food sources for birds, or native wildflowers to attract brilliant hummingbirds and different species of butterflies, moths, or bumblebees as pollinators. A well-planned natural landscape will bring many kinds of wildlife to your garden.

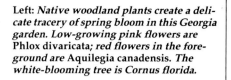

Left: *Native woodland plants create a delicate tracery of spring bloom in this Georgia
garden. Low-growing pink flowers are*
Phlox divaricata; *red flowers in the foreground are* Aquilegia canadensis. *The
white-blooming tree is* Cornus florida.

Below: Cornus florida *forms the understory
in a nearby oak-hickory forest.*

Above: *A Texas gardener created a prairie of bluebonnets (Lupinus) and Mexican primrose. Swaths are mowed to make paths where they are needed.*

Left: *The same flowers carpet a natural Texas prairie as far as the eye can see.*

Preservation and conservation

Growing native plants also makes good sense. First, it preserves in our gardens species that may soon disappear from wild areas as forests are cut down, brushlands cleared, swamps drained, and the natural habitats of native plants otherwise developed for homesites and cities. The native plants of North America abound in rare and little-appreciated beauties; we can help to prevent the tragedies of plant extinction by preserving them in our gardens.

Growing rare native plants in the garden also preserves a habitat for the insects that pollinate their flowers, and the other wildlife species whose life cycles are intertwined with each plant species. Many of our native birds, insects, and larger animals are becoming rare because the plants and natural environments that fed and sheltered them are becoming rare.

Native plant landscapes can also help to conserve scarce resources of energy and water. An expanse of flowering meadow needs mowing only once a year; a bluegrass or fescue lawn needs mowing once a week in the growing season. In those regions of the country that are seasonally dry, planting the native plants of the region ensures tolerance to periodic drought, and allows you to supply much less supplemental water than exotic plants would require. In addition, the plants native to a region are almost always more resistant to the insects and diseases of the region than other plants. Although a greater number of insects and diseases may prey on them, the damage is seldom devastating.

Lower mowing and watering requirements mean that native plant gardens, once they are established, can require substantially less maintenance time and expense than gardens

Top: *The Arizona desert in bloom. The strong lines of rock and cactus are softened by a gray-green carpet of herbaceous plants that includes such colorful bloomers as yellow bitterbrush* (Encilia) *and blue lupines.*

Left: *April in the garden of the Sonoran Desert Museum, located near the wild site pictured above. The landscape has been enhanced by condensing greater variety into less space, and through careful arrangement.*

of exotic plants. It is important to realize that this is not always true; some native species, like some exotic plants, are finicky and specific in their needs, though their rare beauty may justify the trouble. In order to be easy and inexpensive to maintain, a native plant garden must meet two criteria: it must be designed carefully to place each plant species in soil, moisture, and light conditions that meet its specific needs, and the garden must be tended carefully and given extra attention during the first few years after planting. After this period, a well-designed native plant garden may require only periodic seasonal maintenance.

A garden for every need

Wherever you live, you can create a beautiful garden with native plants. As we'll point out frequently in this book, it is important in most cases to use the native plants of your geographic region—these will be best adapted to your garden, and will require the least care. But this need not limit you. Within each region are dozens of plants to fulfill every landscape function from providing overhead shade, to carpeting the ground with greenery, to offering cut flowers for the house. Whether you have a postage stamp garden in the city, a small suburban lot, or a large rural or vacation property, native plants can enhance its beauty and give it a sense of "belonging" to the natural region where you live.

Above right: *Boulders create niches for tufts of green along a high mountain stream.*

Right: *A gardener in the hills north of New York City created a garden version of a mountain stream by using power equipment to arrange rock. The banks are planted with small alpine natives.*

Native plant communities

Plant communities are shaped by relationships between plants, as well as by the climate and soil of the region.

Wherever you live, plants share your life. Maybe it's only a struggling geranium or a hard-bitten tree planted between the city pavements. Maybe, if you live in the suburbs, a remnant remains in your yard of evergreen forests, grasslands, or deciduous woods. Or if you live still farther from the urban centers, you may even know wild places nearby, where the swamps, forests, and wildflowers have been there as long as anyone can remember.

The plants around us, wherever we are, are not isolated individuals, but are in active relationship with other life forms and with their environment. Plants absorb nutrients and water from the soil and gases from the air, and give off other gases to the air and substances to the soil. Plants provide food and shelter for animals and insects, and are in turn pollinated by them, and their seeds distributed. The creatures who eat the plants are in their turn eaten by other animals and insects, called predators. When any plant or animal dies, its remains are consumed by scavengers and *saprophytes* (plants and microorganisms that feed on decaying matter). The nutrients bound up in each plant or animal are then released to the soil and air, and eventually nourish other plants and animals. This web of interactions is called an *ecosystem,* and the

Growth and decay, fallen trees, and new young sprouts are part of the natural ecosystem, as in this Pacific rain forest.

science that studies the ecosystems of the world, the relationships between living things and their environments, is called ecology.

This book is about gardening and landscaping with the plants native to the continental United States. In learning to know and use these plants, we can study each separate plant as an individual, and discover its needs and preferences so it will do well in the garden. This is how we have learned to grow many exotic plants from other parts of the world, with the information gleaned from books, conversations with other gardeners, and trial-and-error in the garden. But with native plants we can do more. Because these plants live and grow near us, we can study them as part of an ecosystem, looking at their relationships with each other, with other life forms, and with their environment. To do this we look at plant *communities;* a plant community is the group of plants that inhabits a particular ecosystem.

The study of native plants as members of plant communities has several advantages. First, because plant communities exist in fairly predictable patterns within geographic regions, we can go out into nature and observe them directly, seeing each plant with its natural companions and observing the temperatures of air and soil at different times of the year, the soil types, moisture levels, and other conditions of its surroundings. Second, we can provide an ideal habitat for a native plant by bringing it into the garden with its natural companions,

in a landscape that imitates nature's design. Because plant communities (and their larger ecosystems) have evolved over long periods to be stable, balanced systems that meet the needs of the plants within them, natural landscaping using plant communities

Below: *This Pennsylvania "moss lawn" was created by clearing the soil and acidifying it with agricultural sulfur — native moss spores did the rest. The lawn must be kept clear of leaves, but is surprisingly tough.*

as a model can provide the ideal growth conditions for each plant of the community, and all can thrive.

When landscaping with native plants, it is essential to choose appropriate plants for your region. The study of native plant communities helps here too. Each region of the country has a different mix of climate and environmental factors: rainfall may be great or little, winter and summer temperatures are very different in the southeast from the northern plains, and soil conditions are highly variable even within regions.

By learning about the plant communities native to your area, you can discover the types of plants that will grow well under the particular environmental conditions there as well as those that will live together in a balanced association. Even if you're just planting a few native wildflowers, getting to know their communities and where they grow will help you meet their needs. Designing a garden around plants native to more distant regions of the United States or other areas around the world will usually make the care of your garden more difficult, for exotic plants may not be well adapted to your local environmental conditions, and could either die an untimely death or require constant nursing to be kept alive. Landscaping with the native plants and communities of your region can create a beautiful garden that fits in with its surroundings, and is easy to care for.

So the first step toward using native plants in your garden is to learn how they occur in natural communities around you. To help you in this, we'll discuss the major plant communities of the United States in this chapter. But first, to explain more about why plant communities exist, how plants come to be associated with each other, and how they interrelate, here is a brief look at some principles of plant ecology.

Plant ecology
Plant ecology is the branch of ecology that looks at relationships between plants and their environment. It is concerned with discovering what types of environments plants live in, how they interrelate with the environment and with each other, and how environments and plant communities change with time.

Habitat and tolerance range
The environment a plant lives in is called a *habitat*. Each habitat is a particular combination of physical, environmental, and *biotic* factors (those factors related to other living organisms). It includes substances such as water and soil; the forces of wind and gravity; conditions such as temperature and light; and other organisms—among them animals, insects, and microorganisms.

Within any large geographic region are many smaller regions with differing conditions of soil, climate, and topography, and within each of these smaller regions are many very different habitats. In the Appalachian Mountains of the eastern United States, for instance, are steep, rocky slopes that support mountain forests of hemlock and fir, rich bottomlands where oak and hickory grow, and abandoned fields of grasses, *forbs* (non-woody broad-leaved plants), and young conifers. And no two of these forests or fields are quite alike as habitats for plant growth. Each has its own particular variations on the basic soils, climate, and topography of the region.

In each habitat are found particular species of plants that are able to grow and reproduce there. A *species* of plants is a group of similar plants that can interbreed and are significantly different from other plant species.

Each species thrives where the combination of factors falls within its "tolerance range." A tree of the eastern deciduous forest, for example, may be able to grow in areas where rainfall is greater than 30 inches a year and falls in both winter and summer, and where temperatures in winter don't fall below 15°F, but will not grow well where rainfall is more seasonal or winter temperatures colder. Each plant species can be shown to have a certain tolerance range for many environmental factors, determining which natural habitats it can grow in and where it can reproduce itself by seed or other means so that its progeny will continue to live there. Some plants, such as the common chokecherry and quaking aspen, have wide tolerance ranges and are found in several types of habitats in diverse regions of the country. Other plants, because of their very narrow tolerances, may be limited to a few scattered stands in one geographic region.

Interactions within the community
Because a number of plants have similar tolerance ranges, they may be found together repeatedly in similar habitats in many parts of a climatic region, forming a recognizable community. Plant communities tend to be regional, because they grow in habitats that are common only in particular regions, due to each region's distinct patterns of climate, soils, and other factors. For instance, certain tall grasses and wildflowers grow together in the tall grass prairie community of the Midwest, in the states of Minnesota, Iowa, Nebraska, Kansas, and Missouri. And the tall sagebrush, often growing with rabbit brush, grasses, and spring wildflowers, is found throughout much of the cold desert region called the Great Basin, in the states of Nevada, Utah, Oregon, and Idaho.

Communities are made up of different kinds of plants, just like those you can see in your garden. *Trees* are woody perennial plants with one main stem or trunk that develops many branches, usually high above the ground. Most trees are over 10 feet tall and have a single trunk. *Shrubs* are low, woody plants with several permanent stems instead of a single trunk. *Forbs* are nonwoody, broad-leaved flowering plants. *Grasses* are members of the grass family, and have long, narrow leaves, jointed stems, flowers in spikelets, and seed-like fruit. *Sedges* are grasslike plants often found on wet ground or in water, having usually triangular solid stems, three rows of narrow, pointed leaves, and very small flowers borne in spikelets. Simpler plants are also found in many communities, including ferns, mosses, and lichens.

These types of plants fit into a definite "social" relationship in any plant community. *Dominant* plants are those species that dominate the community and affect the habitat most, by virtue of their size or numbers. They are frequently the tallest plants in a community, forming the layer called the *overstory*. In a forest or woodland, the dominant plants are trees; in a grassland, grasses; and in the desert or chaparral, usually shrubs. *Subdominant* plants are those species regularly present but in more limited numbers, and are often smaller in size. Subdominant plants often grow in the middle layers of the community, called the *understory*. In the eastern deciduous forest, for example, understory plants include redbud and several species of dogwood.

Additional plant species may appear briefly or only in certain restricted habitats within a plant community. These may occur as occasional trees and shrubs in the understory, or as part of the lowest vegetation layer of the community—the *ground layer*. Some of these species that are neither dominant nor subdominant may still seem to dominate the community at certain times of year or in some habitats. Examples are the blanket of short-lived spring flowers in the desert, or the sphagnum mosses of a northern bog.

The plants in a community aren't independent; they interact with each other in various ways. One of these ways is *competition* between plants. Competition arises because in any environment some substances or factors important to plant growth are limited, such as water in the desert, light in a forest, or nutrients in poor soils. This results in some individual plants being handicapped or eliminated, and in few new species being able to establish a foothold in the community. Competition shapes plant communities and determines their density. For example, intense competition for limited water and soil nutrients is a main reason for the wide and nearly regular spacing of many desert shrub communities.

Another type of interaction between plants is called *allelopathy*, which is the inhibition of one plant's growth by another plant's chemistry. Many plants—among them pines, manzanita, and madrone—produce substances in the soil through their roots or the decomposition of their leaves that make it difficult for most other plants to grow near them.

Other interactions between plants are more beneficial to both sides. Many plants depend upon other (most commonly larger) plants to shade them and provide them with moisture, especially as new seedlings. Larger plants, such as dominant trees in a forest community, can increase the humidity in their environment, and moderate its temperature fluctua-

Above: *Disorder is often a part of the beauty of natural landscapes. These fallen leaves form a colorful mosaic that illustrates the variety of trees that grow in an Eastern mixed deciduous forest.*

tions. Minute fungi called *micorrhizae* (these are plants, too), growing on the roots of conifers in poor soils, help to make soil minerals more available to the trees. It's important to remember that plants are not the only members of ecosystems; they also have interactions with animals, insects, humanity, and other environmental forces. Some of these interactions encourage plant growth and others may eliminate entire plant species.

These positive and negative interactions have evolved in most native plant communities over thousands of years, and the plants of each community have adapted to them, learning to tolerate and depend on each other in a balanced relationship. This means that most native plant communities are self-maintaining, and that gardens based on the native plant communities of a region are usually more stable and require less care than

mixtures of exotic plants.

Native plant communities aren't perfectly uniform. Each broad type of community displays a similarity in the basic plant species, organization in the environment, and general appearance of the community, but within each community of this type, the vertical structure, horizontal pattern, and species mix changes slightly as it responds to varying soil depths, changes in moisture, and differing slopes. Different areas of each community may appear slightly different, and each community may appear slightly different from others of the same type. Thus each small region within the short-grass plains community can be unique in the way the grasses and forbs are arranged, how tall they grow, and when each flowers, even though they all share the same basic species and general appearance.

Plant succession

Plants in a community affect not only each other but also the environment around them. Plants can gradually alter their habitat by bringing about changes in light intensity and quality, humidity, temperature, soil chemistry, soil composition, and soil depth. As the habitat changes, it may come to favor other species, and in time it usually does become unfavorable for the original plants. Some of the changes that occur in most plant communities are a gradual decrease in air movement and a corresponding increase in humidity beneath the layers of vegetation; the accumulation of leaf litter, which adds to the organic content and moisture-holding capacity of the soil; and the moderation of temperatures as the community becomes established.

Plant communities change over time, partly as a result of these changes in their habitat. Some of the changes are temporary. An example is what happens in a forest when a large overstory tree declines and dies. This creates a warmer area with more light, which will allow some of the understory trees to grow larger. Many new spring and summer wildflowers will bloom in this clearing for several years. Changes of this type occur constantly in all communities, but they are usually temporary, as the dominant vegetation eventually reclaims its territory.

A more permanent change in plant communities is *plant succession.* This is the gradual replacement of plant communities in a given area, until a community develops that is in a dynamic equilibrium with the environment and is stable and self-maintaining. Particular types of habitats in a region will usually go through a predictable series of communities (called *seral stages*), until the *climax* stage, or self-maintaining community, is reached. Each of the seral communities brings about changes in the habitat that favor the plants of the next stage, and as a result, each is slowly replaced. This process continues until the climax community, which can maintain a stable habitat for a long period—sometimes thousands of years—is established. An example of plant succession is the succession that occurs as a bog in a northern forest gradually fills in. First, sphagnum mosses grow in the open water, followed gradually by sedges. As the bog begins to fill in, certain acid-tolerant shrubs colonize its edges. Eventually, scattered individuals of black spruce and tamarack move in, followed after centuries by the climax northern forest of spruce and fir. This type of succession, in which a plant community evolves from water, ice, or rock, is called *primary succession*, and occurs very slowly, often over thousands of years.

Another type of succession, called *secondary succession,* takes place after an environment is disturbed, as when a forest is clear-cut for lumber, or a fire kills the native vegetation in an area. It is usually a shorter process. An example of secondary succession is that which occurs in abandoned farm fields in the Piedmont of North Carolina. At first, annual grasses and forbs take over, followed by various perennial flowering plants. Gradually, pine seedlings take root among these and, growing up, become a pine forest. In the cool, shady environment of the forest, oak and hickory seedlings spring up, germinating and growing more successfully than the pine seedlings, and eventually surviving them to dominate the forest. This secondary succession, from open field to oak-hickory forest, may be complete in 50 to 300 years. In some regions, the expected climax stage is unable to develop because the disturbances (fire, logging, and other events) recur regularly, before the climax community is reestablished. An example is the extensive community of various pines and grasses on the coastal plain of the Southeast, which is maintained by frequent fires. Were it not for these fires, the surrounding climax forest of live oak, laurel, and magnolia would probably replace the pines.

When planning your natural landscape, the principles of succession can work for you. If you choose to recreate a plant environment that is the climax community for your region, it will be stable and easy to maintain. However, if you cut out forest trees around your house to establish a meadow, be aware that you are trying to establish an early successional stage within the forested environment, and it will be harder to maintain as the surrounding woods continually try to colonize it. Understanding the patterns of native plant succession in your region can also help you succeed in establishing new plant communities on your property. If you want to establish a particular plant community that grows near you, you can follow nature's method of first planting the dominant species, which will then begin to change the habitat and make it more suitable for later planting of the other members of the community.

Native plant communities

There are dozens of native plant communities in the United States and southern Canada. We'll look first at the climatic regions and major vegetation types in this part of the world, and then at the different plant communities within each type. Because the main focus of this book is growing native plants and plant communities, we've grouped some smaller communities together and focused especially on those most useful to gardeners. The community shown for a particular region of the map is the major community of that area. Each region is really a complex environment; many other communities exist in small pockets, such as meadows within forests and woodlands, tundra on high mountains, coastal communities in narrow bands along the coasts, and various aquatic communities. These smaller communities are limited or scattered so they cannot be easily mapped, but are important in each region.

Vegetation types and climate

The native plant communities of the U.S. can be grouped into broad vegetation types, based on the physical appearance of the community and whether the dominant plants are trees, shrubs, grasses, small alpine plants, or water plants. Climate has strongly influenced the distribution of each vegetation type, but other factors such as soils and human activities are important in many regions.

Forest

Regions of more mild climate, where ample water is available to plants, favor the development of forests. A forest is a vegetation type dominated by trees with a height greater than 15 feet, and with interlocking crowns that cast dense shade on the forest floor. In different forest regions, the dominant trees are evergreen conifers, broadleaf deciduous trees, broad-

Native plant communities of the United States and southern Canada

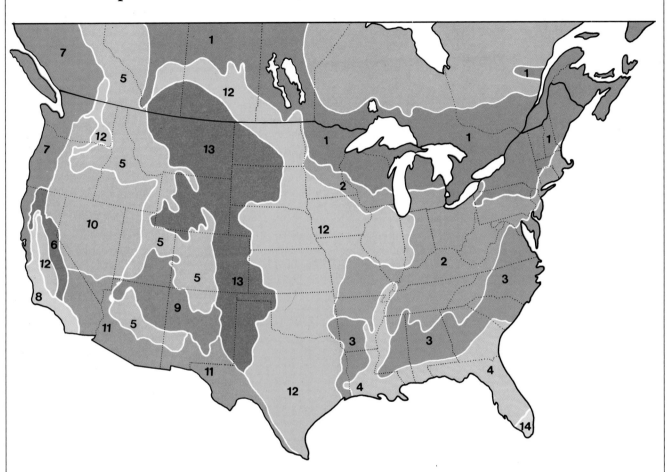

Use this map and descriptions of major plant communities to learn about the native vegetation of your region. Whether you live in the country, the suburbs, or a large city, the map will give you an idea of the vegetation types that are native there and that will tolerate your region's environmental conditions.

FOREST

1. Northern mixed forest
2. Eastern deciduous forest
3. Southeastern mixed forest
4. Outer coastal plain forest
5. Rocky Mountain forest
6. Sierra-Cascade forest
7. Pacific forest

SHRUBLAND AND WOODLAND

8. Coastal chaparral
9. Pinyon-juniper woodland

DESERT

10. Cold desert
11. Warm desert

GRASSLAND

12. Tall-grass prairie
13. Short-grass plains

SUBTROPICAL

14. True subtropical

leaf evergreen trees, or a combination of these. Forest soils are usually shallow but fertile soils, and occur in widely varying climates (although ample rainfall is a constant). Many types of forest are found in the United States and southern Canada: the mixed forests of the Gulf and Atlantic coastal plains, the great eastern deciduous forest, the northern mixed forest of the lake states and New England, and the northern coniferous forest, which stretches in a broad band across Canada.

Northern mixed forest

The forests of New England and the central lake states are primarily of coniferous trees, with widely spaced stands of broadleaf deciduous trees. This plant community can be considered a very wide transition zone between the great coniferous forests of northern Canada (called *Taiga*, these are outside the area covered by this book), and the deciduous forests of the eastern United States. The coniferous forest also occurs on the highest peaks of the Appalachian Mountains to West Virginia and North Carolina.

This area was scoured and shaped by glaciers in ages past, and many of its landforms bear witness to this: the topography is mainly flat plains with occasional low hills or gentle mountains, countless lakes and bogs in shallow depressions, and the great piles of stones called *moraines*.

The climate of this northern region is cool, with a short growing season, and long, often severe winters. Precipitation is evenly spread throughout the year, and is moderate in amount (24 to 45 inches annually). The generally cool temperatures slow evaporation, so plants here experience little water stress.

The major plants of this community are various pines, hemlock, and red cedar, with spruce in cooler areas. Deciduous species are sugar maple, basswood, beech, and paper birch. The conifers form a generally dense, dark forest, so undergrowth is limited by low light and consists mainly of a ground layer of ferns, mosses, and lichens, with scattered small trees and shrubs, such as witch hazel, mountain maple, rhododendron, and dogwood. The patches of deciduous forest are more open, and are bare of leaves in early spring; here and in clearings in the conifer stands are greater numbers of shrubs, and many wildflowers such as Dutchman's breeches, trout lily, wild orchids, wood sorrel, and twinflower.

Eastern deciduous forest

These are the forests of the eastern United States south of the coniferous forests. Their flora is rich and varied. The community is dominated by winter-deciduous trees of many species, and smaller, subdominant trees, shrubs, ferns, and wildflowers.

Deciduous forest covers a large region extending from the lake states and New England in the North, to the Ozarks of Arkansas and Missouri in the West, and south into Georgia and Alabama. Within this area is much topographic variety. In the North (in Indiana, Ohio, and southern Wisconsin), is an area of flat, glaciated plains. Further south are the Appalachian plateaus of Pennsylvania and West Virginia, and the low plateau of western Kentucky.

Although the climate naturally varies within such a large region, it is generally one of milder winters than the northern mixed forest, with a 4- to 6-month growing season and very humid summers. The rainfall of about 40 inches is evenly distributed throughout the year. Soils are rich in humus and slightly acidic in the East, becoming drier and less acid toward the midwestern prairies.

The major deciduous trees of oak, beech, maple, basswood, elm, tulip tree, and ash are found in many combinations in different areas, and can reach 100 feet in height where they are undisturbed. Species of alder, birch, and willow grow on more moist sites, and the scattered understory trees include redbud, shadblow, and dogwood. In early spring, while the overhead trees are still out of leaf and light floods the forest, a lush ground cover of many ferns and wildflowers, including bloodroot, Dutchman's breeches, trout lily, and wood anemone springs up, to die with the increasing shade of summer.

Because this is a region of deep, fertile soils, the forests have been cut and the land used for agriculture in many areas.

Southeastern mixed forest

An open forest of loblolly, shortleaf, and other pines, with an understory of grass, covers much of the southern Atlantic and inner Gulf coastal plains. This land slopes gently toward the coast, and has a mild winter climate, hot humid summers, and precipitation of 40 to 60 inches spread evenly throughout the year. Because of the high precipitation, many soils are nutrient-poor (the frequent rains carry the nutrients below the reach of plant roots), and the water table is often high near the surface. Near the Atlantic coast, the sluggish streams broaden into swamps of gum and bald cypress trees. Stands of oak and hickory, and upland bogs—called *pocosins*—that grow evergreen shrubs such as viburnum, blueberry, and dogwood, are found in some areas.

Frequent fires play a major role in maintaining this community. The pines are more fire-resistant than the other trees and shrubs, and in many areas have as an understory just a ground layer of fire-tolerant grasses.

Outer coastal plain forest

From northern Florida to the Gulf Coast, and inland along the lower Mississippi Valley, is a forest dominated by live oak, laurel, and magnolia species, with a rich understory of tree ferns, shrubs, small palms, and herbaceous plants. Mosses, woody vines, and orchids and other *epiphytes* (plants that grow on trees, but aren't parasites) cling to many of the trees. Extensive stands of pine with an understory of grass are in some areas; cypress-gum swamps are found in the lowlands.

Native palmetto (Serona repens) *grows beneath young pine trees in the Apalachicola National Forest in Florida.*

The climate of this region is like that of the southeastern mixed forest, with equable temperatures and abundant rainfall. Soils are also similar: highly leached of nutrients, wet, and acidic, including both sands and silts.

Rocky Mountain forest

The Rocky Mountains extend from eastern British Columbia and western Alberta south through parts of Washington, Montana, Wyoming, Colorado, Utah, New Mexico, and Arizona. Like other mountainous regions, the climate changes markedly with increasing altitude. Near the base of the mountains the precipitation is only 10 to 20 inches, but increases to about 40 inches on the higher slopes. It occurs mostly in winter, and as snow at higher elevations. The eastern side of the mountains, bordering the Great Plains, is drier than the western slopes. With increasing altitude, the length of the growing season shortens, and temperatures in both winter and summer are lower.

Because of these climatic changes, the Rocky Mountain forest is comprised of distinct vegetation zones, according to elevation. Above timberline is alpine tundra. The highest forest zone begins at timberline (about 11,500 feet in the mid-Rockies). It is a belt of stunted, wind-twisted conifers, blending into a subalpine forest of Engelmann spruce, limber pine, and subalpine fir. Below this, at elevations ranging between about 6,500 feet and 9,000 feet (higher in the south), is a rich, dense forest of Douglas fir and ponderosa pine, often with some stands of lodgepole pine and aspen. A few shrubs, grasses, and herbaceous plants occupy forest clearings.

Sierra-Cascade forest

This forest community is found in the Sierra Nevada and southern Cascade Mountains of California. Much of this region was shaped by glaciers. The steep, precipitous slopes are crossed by deep river valleys; granite peaks rise abruptly above the Great Basin to the east, and fall gently toward the foothills to the west.

As in the Rockies, the climate changes with elevation; precipitation amounts are greater and temperatures are cooler at higher elevations. Both winter and summer are warmer, and rainfall is more seasonal (mostly in winter) at lower elevations.

The Sierra-Cascade forest zones are similar to those of the Rocky Mountains, though the plant species are mostly different. Below the alpine tundra is an open subalpine forest of red fir, mountain hemlock, lodgepole pine, and whitebark pine, with a few shrubs and herbaceous plants in the understory. Below this is the montane forest of Jeffrey pine, Douglas fir, sugar pine, white fir, and incense cedar. Giant sequoia trees grow in isolated groves in the middle-elevation southern Sierra. At lower elevation are open forests of Jeffrey and ponderosa pine with grasses beneath and, below these, the foothill zone of live oak woodlands and chaparral on the west side and the sagebrush of the Great Basin on the east.

Pacific forest

In the steep, rugged mountains of coastal northern California, the northern Cascade Range of Oregon and Washington, and along the nearby coastal plain and valleys grow, dense forests of Douglas fir, western red cedar, hemlock, various firs, Sitka spruce, and—in northern California—the coast redwood. The climate is generally mild in both summer and winter, though it grows more severe inland, particularly on the eastern slope of the Cascades. The precipitation, ranging from a moderate 30 inches in the south to as much as 300 inches on Washington's Olympic Peninsula, can be somewhat seasonal, with more rainfall in the winter. Humidity is high in most areas.

Because of the ample water supply, the forest trees grow very tall and the understory is lush with vine maple, rhododendron, flowering currant, and many other shrubs, perennial wildflowers, ferns, and mosses. Plant growth is richest in the temperate rain forest of Washington's Olympic

Dense coniferous forest is typical of the slopes of the Rocky Mountains. Contrast is provided by the fall color and year-round white bark of quaking aspens.

High humidity and over 200 inches of rain per year create a lush green carpet in the Hoh rain forest of Olympic National Park in Washington State.

Peninsula. In the gentle Coast Ranges of northern California is a forest of broadleaf trees, especially live oak and madrone, with various shrubs in the understory.

Woodland and shrubland

With decreased precipitation, especially in regions where rainfall is highly seasonal, the "reduced forest" vegetation types of woodlands and shrublands appear. A woodland is an open forest: an environment still dominated by trees, but where the trees provide only between 30 percent and 70 percent cover. Woodland trees are not usually the species of forested regions but are often smaller trees, some almost shrubs in size. Because a woodland is an open community with ample light, it usually has many shrubs, forbs, and grasses in the understory. Major woodlands of North America are the pinyon-juniper woodland of the American Southwest and the Great Basin (the area between the Sierra Nevada and the Rockies), and the evergreen-oak woodland of the California chaparral.

Shrublands also occur in these climatic conditions of reduced and seasonal rainfall, and are usually dense growths of broadleaf evergreen shrubs or small, shrublike trees, both with hard, leathery leaves and other adaptations to water stress. Chaparral is an evergreen shrubland in much of southern and central California, and in scattered areas of the Southwest.

Pinyon-juniper woodland

On the deeply cut Colorado Plateau of Arizona, New Mexico, southern Utah, and Colorado grows an open woodland of pinyon pine and several species of juniper. Soils are poor and stony. The woodland trees are small, rarely taller than 30 feet, and scattered. Between the trees grow shrubs of serviceberry, cliffrose, and other species, and a sparse ground cover of short grasses. Because of its elevation (5,000 to 7,000 feet), the climate of the Colorado Plateau varies from other areas of the Southwest: winters are cold and summer days are hot, with cool nights. Temperatures are lower at higher elevations. Rainfall is about 20 inches a year, though local dry areas may only receive 10 inches, and it falls in both summer and winter.

The light rainfall of the California Sierra foothills supports widely spaced evergreen scrub oaks and a spring burst of purple brodiaeas. The plants beneath the oaks become dry and golden from May to October.

Areas that are drier or lower can generally support only a sparse grassland, descending in elevation to the dry desert floor.

Pinyon-juniper woodland is also found as the highest-elevation life zone of the Great Basin, growing on the rocky ridges and low mountains above the sagebrush-clad basins.

Chaparral
Chaparral is composed almost entirely of evergreen shrubs and small trees with hard, leathery leaves. It is found in large areas of the central California coast ranges and mountains of southern California, at elevations from sea level to 8,000 feet. It also occurs in scattered locations in Arizona and other southwestern states. The climate is generally mild in both winter and summer, and precipitation of 12 to 40 inches occurs mainly as winter rain. Summers are hot and dry, and the plants are very tolerant of water stress.

Associated with the chaparral in many areas of California is an open woodland of evergreen oaks, California laurel, and madrone, with an understory of manzanita, ceanothus, toyon, chamise, and various grasses. A *riparian* (stream) woodland of sycamore, alder, and cottonwood grows near streams.

Grassland
In regions where there isn't enough rain to support trees, grassland is found. Grassland is characterized by dominant grasses, though many forbs are also present and may seem dominant when in bloom. Shrubs and trees may also be found in grasslands, but usually only as individuals or groves growing near creeks or where the water table is within reach of their roots. Grassland soils are frequently fertile, and many grasslands of the United States and Canada are now plowed for agriculture. Grasslands historically formed much of the heartland of North America, extending from Texas north into Canada, east to Illinois, and west to the high plains of Wyoming, Montana, and Alberta. Where the great grasslands meet the adjacent forests, they form a vegetation type known as *savanna.* Grasses are dominant in savanna, but trees are regularly present and their canopies may shade as much as 30 percent of the ground. Grasslands are also found as meadows within forests, with shrubs in the arid West, and as coastal prairies along the coasts.

Tall-grass prairie
In a broad band along the western edge of the Eastern deciduous forests, from the eastern plains of Alberta to Texas, were once the tall-grass prairies. Historically, this region included much of the states of Nebraska, Iowa, Kansas, Missouri, Illinois, and Indiana. This is the richest part of the great grassland, a nearly flat region that rises from the eastern forests to the western plains, a region of deep, fertile soils and grasses as tall as a man on a horse. Little of the tall-grass prairie now remains, having given way to the cultivated grasslands of corn, wheat, and other crops.

Rainfall is lower here than in the adjacent forests, and steadily decreases toward the west. Amounts vary from 40 inches in the east to 15 inches in the short-grass plains of the west, and it occurs mainly as summer rain. Winters can be very cold and summers very hot, with hot, drying winds. Plants here must adapt to summer water stress. Soils are heavier than in the forests, and lower in some nutrients.

The appearance of the tall-grass prairie changes from spring to fall. In spring and early summer, forbs such as compass plant send up tall flowering stalks, and dominate with their showy blooms. Gradually, the grasses (including big bluestem, Indian grass, and others) grow taller than the forbs and, in mid-to-late summer, their flowering stems can reach heights of 10 feet and more.

Extensive areas of tall-grass prairie alternating with belts of forest form an area called the *prairie parkland*, a transition zone between grassland and forest that extends from Alberta through Illinois, Missouri, Kansas, and Oklahoma, to the Gulf Coast. The trees of this region include oak, hickory, and, in the north, aspen. At the southern edge of the tall-grass prairie is the *prairie brushland* of Texas, which blends the grasses with mesquite, live oak, and juniper.

In eastern Nebraska and Kansas and in the uplands of Iowa, taller and shorter grasses intermingle in a transition zone between the tall-grass prairie and short-grass plains.

Short-grass plains
With lower rainfall and heavier, less fertile soils, tall-grass prairie gradually diminishes toward the west, blending into the short-grass plains of Alberta, the western Dakotas, Montana, Wyoming, Colorado, and the Texas Panhandle. The elevation of this Great Plains region gradually rises from 2,500 feet in the east to 5,000 feet at the western edge, where it meets the Rocky Mountains. The land surface is broken in some regions

The Jamez river of New Mexico flows through a high cold desert. Poplars, turning yellow in the autumn chill, take advantage of the limited moist zone, while sage dots slopes further from the water.

by canyons, rugged buttes, and tumbled "badlands."

In this semiarid region, the high sod-forming grasses predominant in the tall-grass prairie give way to shorter grasses, many of which are bunchgrasses. These do not provide a hundred percent cover, and they alternate with patches of bare ground.

Many forbs flower in spring and summer, including sunflower, evening primrose, coneflower, and Indian paintbrush. Trees and shrubs are scattered; isolated individuals of bur oak and cottonwood occupy sheltered or moist habitats, and mesquite and cactus are common in some areas, especially in Colorado and Wyoming.

Short-grass plains are found in several other regions of the West. Bordering the warm southwestern deserts in Arizona and New Mexico is an arid grassland of grama grass and other species, dotted with desert shrubs and cacti in open stands. An extensive grassland once covered the Central Valley of California; this may have been mostly species of needlegrass, but is now almost completely agricultural fields and grasslands of imported annual grasses. The Palouse region of eastern Washington and Oregon once supported extensive grasslands of bluebunch wheatgrass, fescue, and bluegrass, intermingled in some areas with Great Basin sagebrush, and the forest trees of the nearby mountains. This area also is now used largely for agriculture.

Desert

In some parts of the western United States, precipitation is very low and irregular, temperatures are high, and strong drying winds are common. Such a climate limits plant growth severely, and here the desert vegetation of widely spaced shrubs and succulent cacti is found. The deserts of the United States are the cold desert of the Great Basin and the warmer deserts of southeast California, Arizona, New Mexico, and west Texas.

Cold desert

The region that includes Nevada, southern Oregon and Idaho, western Utah, and northwestern California is

The giant saguaro cactus at sunset in the Sonoran desert shows dramatic form, a feature typical of desert plants.

Unusual plants abound in the white cedar bogs of South Carolina. Tall yellow pitcher plants nod over floating Arum *leaves.*

composed of numerous interior basins, dissected by steep, parallel mountain ranges. Few streams drain to the coast. The region is at fairly high elevation (near 5,000 feet), and some of its mountains rise 2,000 feet above the basin floors. This is an area of little precipitation; rainfall amounts range from 5 to 20 inches, mostly in winter. Summers are hot, and winters moderately cold. Frost may occur in any month of the year.

The major plant, growing in widely spaced, open stands on the poor soil, is tall sagebrush. A number of other shrubs are dominant in moist areas, strongly alkaline soils, or soils with high salt concentrations, including rabbit brush, shadscale, and saltbush. Few trees are present in the basins, although pinyon-juniper woodland grows at the higher elevations in the mountains. Many short-lived annual flowers germinate and bloom after the heavy rains.

Warm desert
This community includes several deserts in the southwestern states: the Mojave of southeastern California, the Sonoran of Arizona and northern Mexico, and the Chihuahuan of southern New Mexico, west Texas, and Mexico. Although their climates are similar, there are some differences, and each area supports slightly different desert vegetation. Rainfall in all three areas is very low and irregular. It falls mainly as erratic winter rains in the Mojave Desert, winter and summer rains in the Sonoran Desert, and primarily as summer storms in the Chihuahuan Desert. In some areas, no appreciable rain may fall for two years. Winters are moderate with occasional frost, except for the Mojave, which has cold winters. Summers are very hot, with extremely high evaporation (and therefore high water stress for plants).

Soils in the lowest areas are fine-textured, heavy, and often have high concentrations of salts. In the *arroyos*, or desert washes, soils may be coarse and gravelly. Soil is almost nonexistent in many areas of the rocky desert

mountains. Most desert soils are highly alkaline and often have a layer of cementlike *caliche* at fairly shallow depth, making growth difficult for most plants.

The Mojave Desert, like the nearby Great Basin, is primarily a landscape of low, scattered shrubs. Creosote bush is widespread. The taller Joshua tree occasionally breaks this pattern, as do scattered cacti. Following the winter rains, many annual flowers bloom, forming a low carpet of bloom in early spring. The plants of the Sonoran Desert are more varied, including the tall saguaro cactus and ocotillo, along with creosote bush and other low shrubs. Arroyos may support some tree growth, particularly paloverde and mesquite. The Chihuahuan Desert is dominated by the low creosote bush, with tarbush, whitethorn acacia, and other shrub companions. These are joined by taller species of yucca, mesquite, and ocotillo in some locations, and by small succulent cacti.

Subtropical region
The southern tip of Florida lies near enough to the tropics to share the tropical wet-dry climate of the Caribbean. In this region, rain falls mainly from late spring to mid-fall, and the winter months are usually dry. Year-round mild temperatures make possible the growth of many tropical plants found nowhere else in·the continental United States.

There are basically two seasons: a long, hot, wet summer (May to September); and a dry, cooler winter and spring (November to March). Cold winter temperatures restrict the distribution of tropical species, and most tropical species grow in a "coastal horseshoe," south of Pinellas County and northern Brevard County.

Southern Florida has a number of distinctive plant communities, with intermingled tropical and temperate vegetation. There are five major plant communities.
Marshes: Much of southern Florida is dominated by fresh and salt water marshes. The predominant plants in both types of marshes are grasses, sedges, and rushes. Saw grass and soft-rush, beak-rush, and Southern wildrice are typical of the inland fresh water marshes. Salt-meadow cordgrass, glasswort, saltmarsh bulrush, and needle rush are common in the brackish and salt marshes found along the coast.
Mangroves: Mangrove forests in coastal brackish or salt water areas.
Hammocks: Evergreen hardwood species consisting mostly of tropical trees. These are "tree islands," surrounded by other vegetation types, usually pineland or swamp. Hammocks are often found where fire protection is given (pinelands burn frequently), on deeper soils. "High" hammocks are drier, and "low" hammocks are wetter, with different species growing in each type.

This peaceful New England river scene reminds us that still or slow-moving water can delight us with reflections of the beauty on its shores.

Pinelands: These pine forests consist of mostly slash pine and saw palmetto, with low shrubs, forbs, and fire-resistant grasses. They are maintained by frequent fire.

Cypress, bay, and willow "heads": Also "tree islands," but of temperate species such as baldcypress, sweet bay, and various willows.

Coastal scrub: Trees and shrubs tolerant of high amounts of bright sun, salt spray, and sea breezes.

Aquatic communities

The presence of the ample water provided by a pond, lake, river, or swamp creates a special habitat for plants, usually softening the stresses common to the surrounding region. Here various types of aquatic vegetation grow: water-dwelling plants such as sedges, water grasses, and cattails, and trees such as bald cypress. Nearby are many land plants adapted to constantly wet soil. The range of plant species and their numbers in aquatic areas varies with the temperature of the water and other factors.

Many types of aquatic communities are found in the United States and southern Canada. Thousands of bogs and lakes punctuate the glaciated forest region of the northern Midwest; small streams and larger rivers flow through the forests and cities of the East and West to the coasts; near the Atlantic and Gulf are great swamps of cypress and gum trees; and desert arroyos mark the underground watercourses of the arid West.

Water provides a habitat for specialized plant communities. Aquatic plants grow in it, and lush growths of shrub and forest often surround it. In many areas, these aquatic communities are of species and vegetation types that would otherwise fare poorly, such as the mesquite of desert washes, or the riparian forests of the plains and prairies.

Lakes can be rich or poor habitats for plants, according to the water depth, acidity, temperature, and the amount of nutrients and oxygen. Warm, shallow lakes can support many water plants, including pondweeds, arrowhead, rushes, and reeds.

Because a swift stream doesn't allow nutrients to collect or plants to root, and is usually cold, few plants live in the water. But it often supports a rich riparian forest or woodland on its banks, with such species as hemlock, alder, birch, willow, cottonwood, and various shrubs.

The riparian forests of the midwestern prairies extend far into the grasslands; those of the California chaparral country grow tall and dense.

Closer to the coasts, streams flow into great, slow-moving rivers. Here the water is warmer, deep silt has collected on the floodplains, and many aquatic plants grow, among them algae, pondweed, and lotus. Along the banks grow tall willows, cottonwoods, sycamores, or other riparian trees adapted to the region.

The arroyos of the desert are a unique environment. They usually contain water only for brief periods following the unpredictable heavy desert rains, but some moisture may remain for an extended period below ground. The various shrubs and trees, that grow in the gravelly arroyo soil, have root systems that can reach deep to tap water far underground.

A swamp is a wetland dominated by trees. The major swamps in the United States are found along the southern Atlantic and Gulf coasts, and in the lower Mississippi Valley. Giant bald cypress trees, festooned with Spanish moss, share this habitat with various species of ash, maple, and tupelo, and many water plants.

Freshwater marshes are a major landscape feature of southern Florida, and are found elsewhere in widely scattered locations. A freshwater marsh is a very rich habitat for many types of plants, including reeds, water grasses, and sedges, all of which provide an ideal habitat for various birds and animals.

Alpine tundra

High in the mountains of the West, and on the tallest peaks of New England, alpine tundra grows at the upper limits of plant growth. The growing season is very short (often less than 2 months) and cool, with

Bright Rydbergias *dapple alpine tundra in the Colorado Rockies. Alpine flowers are generally low growing, an adaptation to the short summer, strong winds, and thin rocky soil where they must survive.*

temperatures rarely exceeding 50°F. Frosts may occur at any time of year.

Tundra occurs as the highest life zone, above the subalpine forests and the last few twisted conifers. Within this zone are various environments: steep slopes, upland meadows, rocky fell fields, and ridgetops. Plants grow in a one-layered community of low, trailing perennials. Species include many dwarf species of willow and other woody shrubs, along with sedges and grasses in the meadows and perennial flowering plants. This flora varies in different regions.

Coastal strands and rocky shores

The climate of coastal regions is generally mild, with temperature moderated by the ocean, and usually with adequate rainfall. But this environment can also be stressful for plants, with its constant wind, salt spray, and generally poor, sandy soils.

Along the Atlantic and Gulf coasts is a broad, gently sloping coastal plain, backed in many areas by extensive dunes. Plants on these coasts may grow in several habitats: beach, tidal land, dune, and swamp. In many areas of the Atlantic Coast, the plant growth must adapt to a very high water table. Parts of the Maine coast are quite rocky. The Pacific Coast has little coastal plain; in many areas, the steep, forested coastal mountains come right to the rocky headlands above the surf.

Major plant species of the Atlantic and Gulf coasts include many grasses, various alders, bayberry, goldenrod, several legumes, and, of course, seaweeds. The Pacific Coast is drier, especially in the south, and supports grasslands, sagebrush, coyote brush, wild buckwheat, sand verbena, lupines, and saltgrass, merging into the Pacific forest in the Northwest.

In regions of persistent sea winds, coastal plants may resemble the plants of the alpine tundra: wind-sheared, twisted, and dwarfed.

Like alpine areas, rocky coasts often support only low plants, due to thin soil, salt spray, and wind. The homes in this California coastal community take advantage of the dramatic terrain and native coastal flora.

Ecotones

Because no plant community or formation is isolated within nature, the formations listed above are frequently found in combination, especially where a great expanse of one vegetation type meets another. There is rarely any clean dividing line, but instead a broad belt where the two formations combine. These transition zones are called *ecotones*. Savanna is an ecotone between grassland and forest; other ecotones occur between all neighboring communities, such as the shrub-dotted desert grassland between the Great Plains grasslands and the Southwest desert, and the open stands of ponderosa pine and sagebrush at lower elevations of the western mountains.

Designing a native garden

A landscape that follows nature's design does not need to exclude people. Your natural landscape should still offer your family the amenities they wish from their garden.

Plants contribute to our lives in many ways. They feed us, shade us from the summer sun, protect us from harsh winter winds, and grace our living environments with flower, fragrance, and form.

The native plants of your region, planted in a well-designed, thoughtful arrangement in the garden, can do all these things. They can also express in your landscape the essential character of the region where you live, as the saguaro cactus and Joshua tree evoke the Southwestern desert, and brilliant autumn maples symbolize the Eastern deciduous forest.

This chapter tells you how to design your natural garden, using native trees, shrubs, ground covers, and wildflowers to create areas for outdoor activities, structure your landscape, control climate and erosion, and bring special beauty to the garden. It shows you how to analyze the possibilities of your landscape site and your family's needs.

Gardens, after all, are for people. And your garden should be for you. The fact that it will be modeled after a natural landscape doesn't mean that you can't entertain in it, or that your children can't play there. Even if you are planning to change only a small part of your yard, take into account how that part will be used. A rustic bench placed in a small grove in the

corner of the yard might make the difference between a corner that is only visited occasionally and a haven for quiet reading or meditation at the end of a busy day.

Landscape analysis

The process of investigating the possibilities is called *landscape analysis.* We are using the term to mean an analysis of the native landscape you wish to recreate, of the garden site, and of the uses to which the garden will be put.

Landscape analysis is divided into several steps. The first is an exploration of the plant communities of your local area. As you spend some time walking through the woods, prairies,

or open shrub communities near your home, you will see how the regional communities discussed in the previous chapter are represented in your own locale. The second step is to ask yourself a set of questions. The answers will help you decide what kind of natural garden you want, and how you'll use it. Finally, you'll look at the important features of your site, to learn what possibilities and limitations it offers.

This process of detailed analysis is especially important if you're planning a large natural landscaping project; it will help you to base the garden's design on a thorough knowledge of your own wants and needs and an understanding of your

A woodland garden can offer quiet paths for strolling, clearings for sitting, privacy from neighbors and a connection with seasonal rhythms.

Native gems, like this yellow native orchid, lady's slipper, charm us as much as do more common flowers we plant for garden color. The blue flower is Phlox divaricata.

site's character. The process is also important if you are just sowing a few wildflowers or planting a small grove of native trees, because it will help you determine the kind of native plants you want to use, the conditions of soil and microclimate in the part of your property where they'll be planted, and the native species that will work well for you. In this case, you'll analyze things on a smaller scale, looking at individual native plant species and their specific habitats in nature, and the site conditions of small areas. Take the time to explore the wider communities the plants live in, and study your site as an organic whole, so that your small planting looks natural and harmonizes with other plantings on the site.

Exploring native communities

From the discussion of major plant communities in the previous chapter, you have an idea of the predominant plant communities of your region. Now go out and explore the natural areas near you, to discover more directly how the native plants of your region grow together in communities, the character of each community, and its habitat. This process will help you gather ideas for your garden.

Native animals, like this toad sitting under a foamflower, help control insects in native environments.

Finding unchanged natural areas near you may not be easy. Many areas may be full of exotic weeds or litter, perhaps overused and unattractive. Try to find a rich, exciting area of nearly all native species, undisturbed for many decades—a forest meadow filled with wildflowers, a richly varied chaparral and oak woodland community, a restored prairie. Local, state, or national parks in many regions of the country preserve native plant communities almost intact. Find other local natural areas by asking native plant gardeners or inquiring at local nurseries. An especially good source of information can be your state native plant or wildflower society or, if your state does not have one, the native plant society of a neighboring state in your region. The society may be able to tell you of nearby native plant communities you can visit, and give you the names of members who are experts on the use of native plants in the landscape. See page 93 for a listing of some native plant societies.

Once you've located native plant communities to visit, you'll need a good pair of walking shoes and a field guide to the plants of your region. Ideally, you might visit different natural areas during several seasons of the year, noting the types of habitats there, what types of plants and species grow in each (use the field guide), and how the community changes with the season. Notice how the plants grow. What are their vertical and horizontal patterns? How are

Native plant communities

Where do you go to see native plant communities? Local, state, and national parks of your region are one place; many of these contain unique and vanishing plants and plant communities. Your region may also have large wildlife sanctuaries or nature preserves, which are often relatively undeveloped natural environments.

Local and state conservation organizations can also help you find natural plant communities to explore. Among these are native plant societies (see listing on page 93), and the Nature Conservancy, a nonprofit organization. The goal of the Conservancy is preservation of native plants and plant communities; most states have a chapter offering regular meetings, lectures, and tours of natural areas.

Many universities have excellent arboretums and botanical gardens on their grounds or nearby. Some of these are dedicated to native North American plants and contain extensive natural areas.

they spaced? What plants grow together? What about the soil: how moist is it? Does it seem fertile? Take notes on the patterns of growth in the community, and on soils, moisture, temperatures, and anything else that seems important, and compare them to your own site. These don't need to be precise measurements, just your impressions. Exploring local natural areas not only gives you knowledge about what grows where and how, but it can also help you learn what you like in a landscape. Note which natural areas seem most attractive to you, what plants and plant groupings you would like to try in your own garden, and what plants in each community seem unattractive.

Defining your ideal landscape

The next part of the process is introspective: the visualization of your ideal landscape. Remember your favorite landscapes—those you have recently explored or others known long ago: the creek where you fished as a child, the dry grass and oaks of the hills that you walked through in summer, or the beach where you spent a winter weekend. You needn't limit your recollections to natural landscapes; think also about beautiful gardens you've visited, what it was like to stroll quietly beneath the trees, how brilliantly the flowerbeds and lawn shone in the sun, the soft forms and colors of a rock garden. Try to define what it was that was beautiful about each of these places—color, plant form, soft shadows, the warmth of the sun, or anything else—and make brief notes for later reference.

With this for inspiration, consider what kind of natural garden you want. Whatever the size of your project, what should its character be? Should it be a forest, a flowery meadow, a desert oasis, a riparian woodland? What features will make this garden a special place? Make notes on the types of plants to include in the garden, the quality of light and shadow, the kinds of spaces and paths, and any other qualities which seem to you essential.

You'll need to temper this vision with a practical knowledge of the kinds of natural environments that can be created in your region, and what plants will grow and thrive there. The discussion of regional

The garden you design may reflect memories of recent weekend trips to the mountains or memories of hours spent trying to outsmart fish when you were a child. A small pond can represent a lake, or a rock garden can represent a mountain.

plant communities in the last chapter will help you in this, indicating the large regions of the country where forest is able to grow, where chaparral communities predominate, and where the scattered shrubs, trees, and cacti of the desert are best adapted. By learning how these regional communities grow in your local area, you'll have an idea of what is possible.

We've talked about patterning your natural landscape after the native plant communities of your area. Though it will be easiest to establish and maintain your landscape if you use the plants native to your area, bear in mind that your garden needn't precisely duplicate any community. Instead, the community can serve as a model and inspiration for your own planting. You can use the major plants of the community in a way similar to their arrangement in nature, but you may wish to shape areas for certain uses, to emphasize showy plantings of your favorite species, or in some other way to intensify the beauties of nature to create your ideal garden.

Analyzing your site

The next step in landscape analysis is to take a critical look at your site. First look at the yard as a physical environment, considering especially those factors important to plant growth: its climate, moisture, and soils.

Begin this study by drawing a base plan. Measure the layout of your yard, where the house sits on the lot, and the locations of garage, outbuildings, fences, patios and other paved areas, paths, and major plants. Convert each measurement in the landscape to inches on your plan, according to the scale you're using.

Now use the guides below to analyze the climate, topography, soils, and existing vegetation of your site. Map the information you gather on overlay tracings of the base plan.

Climate

Now gather information on the climate of your geographic region and local area. The regional averages of precipitation (rainfall and snowfall), temperature, and wind set the basic pattern for the entire geographic area. But, within this, each smaller area varies somewhat. Your locale may have more rainfall than other parts of the region and milder temperatures at all seasons, or it may experience more extreme summer heat and winter cold and less summer rain. Either way, you will need to take your local climate into account when selecting native plants for your garden.

The climate of your site will also have its own distinct patterns. Your site will, in fact, be made up of a number of small, distinct climate zones called *microclimates*: some site areas are more windy, hot, and dry than others, which could be more moist, cooler in summer, and warmer in winter. These areas, each having its particular soil characteristics, form the plant habitats of your site. It is important in most cases to match the native plants you choose to the existing habitats of your site, but you can also use plantings to slowly modify a habitat, making it more moist, cool, or humid as the plants grow to maturity.

Obtain information on regional and local precipitation amounts and temperatures. The chamber of commerce in most towns has a table of temperature and precipitation based on National Weather Service data. Obtain information on the microclimates of your site through your own observations at different times of the year. Record your climate and microclimate information as outlined areas with notes on an overlay drawing of your base plan.

Soils

Soils are highly variable even within local areas; within your yard you may have several soil types. Soil *pH* (its acidity or alkalinity), fertility, drainage, and moisture content can be critical to the survival of native (and exotic) garden plants. Certain problems, such as accumulations of salts or toxic metals in the soil or a shallow layer of the cementlike hardpan common in the West, can make plant growth very difficult if not corrected.

To obtain basic information on your soil—texture, degree of compaction, wet and dry areas, and depth—make your own observations. You will find out a great deal by digging several holes. This will tell you what type of soil you have, whether it's clay or sandy, and if there are layers of different types of soil under the surface layer. Check drainage by filling these holes with water. Let them sit overnight, then fill the holes again and see how fast the water level drops. If it drops more slowly than ¼ inch per hour, you should consider improving the drainage. If it drops more rapidly than that, you probably won't have drainage problems.

The inexpensive soil test kits available at garden centers offer a quick check of soil pH. For a more accurate analysis, ask your county agricultural extension agent or the Soil Conservation Service to recommend a labora-

A landscape plan tells you how much space you have, helping to avoid costly errors. After you have studied your garden space and tried to visualize changes, draw new garden details to scale around diagrams of existing structures.

Landscape plans

A landscape plan is a way of representing your property on paper. Usually it's drawn as though you were looking down on your house and lot from an airplane: trees, shrubs, and other plants are indicated as circles, paths as parallel lines, and structures as flat geometric shapes. If you are doing a large landscape project, or one that includes new structures such as an outbuilding or arbor, the plan should be drawn to scale, which means that one inch on the plan should equal a fixed number of feet measured in the landscape. Typical scales for landscape plans are 1 inch = 4 feet (to show small areas in large size), and 1 inch = 16 feet (to show larger areas). If your project consists of just a few new plantings, a small sketch plan will suffice; this need not be drawn to scale, but should show the approximate layout of the area and its plants.

To draw landscape plans, you will need a roll or several sheets of drafting paper (24 by 36 inches is a good size), a roll of tracing paper of the same size, several drafting pencils of grade F or B, a ruler or architect's scale, a smooth table or drafting board, masking tape to attach the paper to the table, and a 25-, 50-, or 100-foot tape for measuring your yard or planting area.

You'll use several types of plans in designing your natural garden. The first is a base plan of your lot showing fixed features and important structures. Overlays are another type of plan. These are handy for recording notes, sketches, and diagrams, as you're working out the landscape design. They are made by tracing the base plan onto drafting or tracing paper. Use overlays to record notes from your site analysis and ideas for new garden uses and, later, to work out schematic landscape plans. Your final plan will usually be drawn on a copy of your base plan and will give complete details of plant species, size, and spacing, and notes on site and soil preparation. For more information on drawing a base plan, overlays, and other landscape plans, see Ortho's book *All About Landscaping.*

tory in your state or region that does soil testing. The agricultural universities in many states test soil without cost or for a nominal fee. Contact the lab for instructions on how to collect the samples. If you live in an arid part of the Midwest or West, have the lab test for soil salts at the same time. The laboratory will tell you what the results mean and give you suggestions for improving the soil.

Map the information on an overlay of your base plan. Note especially the locations of areas with shallow, poor, or rocky soil, spots that dry rapidly or stay wet for long periods, and any special problems.

Vegetation

Existing vegetation and its condition can give you hints about the plant habitats of your site, suggesting which are moist and fertile, where soil is poor or shallow, and even the patterns of the prevailing winds. If you are planning major landscaping with native plants, it's important to assess the condition of each existing plant of significant size to decide whether or not to keep it.

It's not necessary to rip out all your existing exotic trees and shrubs if you are planning a natural landscape, especially if they are doing well and are attractive. Growing new shrubs and trees to replace mature plants can take many years and can be costly.

Map important existing vegetation on your site analysis overlay—both the plants you plan to keep and those to be removed. For those plants you decide to save, consider whether they will thrive under the same conditions as the native plants they will be growing next to, and how they will look in a landscape of native plants.

How you use your garden

In visualizing your ideal landscape, you defined your aesthetic vision of the garden. In the last section, you looked carefully at the physical environment of your site. Now look at your practical needs. What do you want to use your site and garden for? Will your garden be a place for relaxing, strolling, and other quiet

pursuits? Should it also include areas for games or entertaining, special collections of native plants, or outdoor work centers? What other garden activities or interests are important to you? If your landscaping project is small, involving only the planting of native shrubs and trees in some parts of an existing garden, look most critically at those parts of the garden. How will you use each area? How can the plants be arranged to serve this purpose? Think about how you use the garden at present, and how you would like to use it.

What kinds of work do you do in your garden? They may be limited to the routine maintenance tasks of weeding, pruning, and watering. Or you may enjoy special horticultural projects such as potting, transplanting, or greenhouse work. What other kinds of work do you do in the garden? New projects to plan for may include a display garden for a native plant collection, or a larger tool shed.

What about play and relaxation? Do you enjoy a quiet stroll along the garden paths in the evening, and

sharing quiet moments in the garden with your family and friends? Perhaps you also like to give large parties and formal dinners on the patio. Does your garden include areas for active games, such as a tennis court, swimming pool, or croquet lawn?

Your garden plantings can also provide privacy and separation, both from neighboring houses or structures and within the garden. Can you feel completely private and secluded in your garden when you wish to? What areas need more separation between them, and what edges of the property need more screening from neighbors or nearby structures? Are there some plants in the garden which screen too much, such as a tall hedge that blocks a view?

Think about how your garden contributes to your feeling of security in your home. What makes you feel safe and secure is very individual; for some it means being able to see every inch of the garden, and for them a garden with no plants other than low ground covers and overhead trees may be most comforting. Others sim-

This Texas patio uses native live oaks and virginia creeper along with exotic foliage plants.

A hidden corner with a rough wood bench invites one to contemplate the beauties of bleeding heart (left rear) and a pale pink native geranium in this Long Island garden. Be sure to give yourself and others vantage points from which to admire details and vistas.

plants of your region, the features of your site, and your landscaping needs. This process is never really complete: you can spend years getting to know the plant species of your area. Also, you'll come to know your site more intimately as you work the soil and establish your natural garden, and your needs will change as time goes on. But you now have a good idea of what you want in a landscape, and you're eager to design and plant it. In the next section, we'll discuss how to design with native plants and the steps in putting together your planting scheme.

Working with your site

Ultimately, your site and its location determine the type of native plants and plant communities you can grow. The basics of the site—landforms, soil type, and climate—are not easily changed. The simplest way to grow native plants is to choose those species that will do well in your site.

But you can also make some changes in your site: reshaping the topography, improving the soil's fertility, and modifying microclimates to improve it as a habitat for the native species of your region and to enable you to grow certain marginally adapted species that you value.

If your site is located in or near an undisturbed natural area, it may already be an ideal habitat for the native plants of your region. Perhaps it is nestled in a deep forest, surrounded by native chaparral, or maybe it overlooks the desert floor. The land may be almost unchanged from its natural state if it has been logged or farmed so many years ago that it has revegetated, or if the only native vegetation removed was a small plot near the house.

On this kind of site, change as little as possible. Develop your natural garden by analyzing the site and studying its soils and microclimates and the different plant habitats these form. Then choose plants from regional communities that grow in similar habitats. If some areas of the site can be made more suitable for certain native species with relatively minor changes in soil fertility, pH, or drainage, make them. This strategy of minimum change will preserve the essential character, or "genius" of your site, and avoid upsetting the delicate balance of slope, drainage,

ply eliminate tall, dense plantings near the house entry. Consider what features of your current garden help you to feel secure and which you'd like to change.

Plants can help control the microclimates of your site. Tall deciduous trees can provide summer shade and coolness, and allow the winter sun to warm the house or patio. Plants can maintain higher humidity in hot, dry climates. Trees and shrubs can be planted to divert wind or to channel welcome breezes. What changes in your existing landscaping would make your garden more pleasant at all times of the year?

Many people plant native plants to simplify landscape maintenance. The planting of a few native species in a garden does not guarantee low maintenance but, once it is established, a natural garden patterned after the native plant communities of an area can often get by with less maintenance than a formal garden of exotic

plants. Take a look at the maintenance requirements of your present landscape. What plants and areas require a great deal of pruning, fertilizing, or watering? Chances are that your lawn is among them, along with any large groupings of plants exotic to your region. If these plants are successful where they are, and you enjoy them, there's no reason to replace them with native species, but you may wish to replace any particularly troublesome plants in difficult locations with native plants well adapted to that situation.

Make notes about the changes you want to make in garden use patterns. List the improvements needed in garden layout and circulation patterns, new activity areas wanted, exotic plantings to replace with native species for easier maintenance, and additional plantings needed for screening or climate control.

This is the end of your landscape analysis. You've looked at the native

This garden in Washington, D.C., shows how plant choice and placement can suggest a native planting. In this case, only the yucca plants (center and left) are natives. *The grass in the rear (*Calamagrostis epigeous*) is a useful European grass that gives the impression it is a native. It is easy to grow and doesn't produce seed, so it isn't invasive.*

vegetation, and animal life that has developed there.

Such undisturbed sites are rare. Far more common is the suburban parcel or urban lot that has lost its natural topography, vegetation, and topsoil to the bulldozer, been compacted during home construction, and is planted with a haphazard mix of plants from all over the world. You can plant native species there too but, before you do, you will usually need to improve the soil, correct problems caused during construction, and make changes to approximate the natural habitats of the native plants you want to grow.

On a more developed site, the changes required to make it suitable for native plants may be extensive. Soil improvement is particularly important for many natives, especially those of woodland or forest origin, which require a fertile, rich, deep, and open soil very unlike that around most homes. Other problems you may need to solve include stabilizing steep slopes or other erosion-prone areas, loosening surface soils, and correcting drainage problems such as water collecting beneath the house or in landscape areas.

Certain types of natural gardens will require more site modification than others. Gardens built near the seacoast must often contend with sandy, nutrient-poor soils. Desert soils also are often poor, and may in addition have accumulations of toxic salts or a rock-like layer of hardpan near the surface. You'll need to improve these conditions for your native plants to thrive. Rock garden plants usually demand loose, gritty soil with excellent drainage, and this requires major changes on many sites.

Planting design

Planting design is the art of arranging plants in the landscape to shape it for our use, comfort, and pleasure, and to enhance the beauties of the site and conceal its faults. Good planting design integrates the various areas of a garden into a unified whole.

The first principle of successful planting design is to use each plant where it will grow and thrive. This involves learning the needs of each plant, the conditions of each part of your garden, and matching one to the other. This task is simplified by the use of native plants that are well adapted to your region, and to the particular light intensities, soil types, and moisture levels of your site.

In this way, designing with native plants is not different from designing with exotic plants: both require positioning each plant and plant grouping where it will succeed and serve its intended purpose in the landscape. But there is one important difference in working with native plants, especially when designing a garden or a planting area that will grow many native species together: the entire composition should appear natural.

Imitating nature's design

What makes a garden look natural? Some gardens seem to evoke nature so well that we feel that nature, not the gardener, created them. You can bring about this effect by using plants exotic to your region, but it can be achieved more easily and effectively by designing with the plants native to nearby hills, prairies, or forests. These plants can be selected and arranged in a garden to express the essence of the natural area through their forms, the pattern of the plantings, the colors of flower and leaf, plant textures, and other qualities.

The easiest way to create a natural-looking planting design is to use the dominant plants of a native plant community as its backbone. Because most gardens are small—especially those in urban and suburban settings—you may not have room to recreate an entire plant community, but you can suggest it by using its dominant plants, arranged as they are in nature. To suggest a forest, plant the dominant forest trees of your region, whether they are the white oak and hickory of the East, the live oak and magnolia of the Southeast, or the conifers of the Pacific slope. The common bunch- and sod-forming grasses of the prairies, combined with a few of the most striking forbs that naturally grow with them, will express the essence of the prairie. In the same way, you can use the most characteristic shrubs of the desert or chaparral, and the low-growing mat plants of alpine environments, as the central plantings of other types of natural gardens.

Use these dominant plants and the other living and non-living elements in your natural garden to symbolize the natural environment you're recreating. Try to sense the essence of the plant community and build your garden to embody it. The Japanese have used this principle for centuries to create beautiful, concentrated expressions of nature's beauty. To do this in your garden, you may want to emphasize certain natural features, exaggerating their usual scale or appearance slightly, to symbolize a plant community. Note how the landforms of the natural community are shaped, what plants commonly grow in close association with each other, and how other elements, such as large stones, are positioned. Symbolize these relationships in the garden by creating small slopes or stream channels, positioning a few stones carefully in harmony with nearby plants to emphasize the topography, or bringing out any other attractive features of the natural community that you are imitating.

Physical characteristics

To use and combine native plants well in your design, you should also study their essential physical characteristics—which include form, color, and texture—and learn how these characteristics change with different times of day and seasons of the year. Learning about these visual qualities of native plants will enable you to express the essence of the natural environment you are recreating. You can design a beautiful arrangement of native plants that will provide year-round centers of interest in the garden, eye-catching contrasts, and repeated elements that give the whole garden unity.

Plan your garden to emphasize the dynamic, changing qualities of plants. Form, color, and texture can change rapidly in plants, especially due to wind, rain, or changes in light. Some conifer trees sway and dance in a breeze; other trees (such as the quaking aspen) tremble and give off a soft, watery sound. The wet glossy leaves of shrubs and trees reflect the sun brilliantly. Plants also change from one season to another. Beds of

A garden can be planned for both winter and summer interest. This expression of a native prairie theme uses native little bluestem grass (in winter foreground) and a yellow Rudbeckia (at back of summer view) *along with exotics that create biseasonal interest.*

short-lived spring wildflowers spring to life, flower, and then disappear with the advent of summer. Deciduous trees and shrubs shed their leaves in autumn, changing the character of the landscape.

Plant groupings

We have discussed some visual qualities of individual plants. Observe also the way that plants are arranged together in nature. Study the plant communities of your area to see how masses of plants are arranged in soft shapes, how woodland paths flow in gentle curves, how the desert is bisected by arroyos, and how smaller plants, larger plants, stones, and landforms fit together. Observe the horizontal patterns of the plant community. These patterns may be quite varied, but each community has its characteristic patterns, usually determined by the way in which its plants reproduce. Trees, shrubs, and grasses that reproduce mainly by seed appear in random, scattered patterns in the landscape. Those that propagate by running roots and the formation of suckers are found in ever-expanding clumps, spreading outward from the parent plant. Other factors may also determine the horizontal pattern of a natural community; the apparently random, widely spread distribution of many desert plants, for instance, is due to intense competition for scarce water and nutrients.

Native plants are also arranged in the vertical patterns called *stratification*. Each plant species occupies a position in the overstory, understory, shrub, or ground layer. Note especially the numbers, distribution, and placement in the vertical strata of those species you plan to use in your garden. By duplicating this arrangement in the garden, you can make the plant look as though it grew there naturally, and also match some of the light, moisture, and soil conditions of its natural habitat.

Edible plants

One further consideration deserves mention here: the leaves, fruits, and seeds of native plants can provide food. Although most of the food plants we prize are highly developed hybrids of exotic species, some native plants such as blueberry, huckleberry, and persimmon provide delicious fruit. The berries or fruits of many others—such as chokecherry, cranberry, and crabapple—can make fine jelly, preserves, or wine. Still other native plants have small and apparently unpalatable fruits, but are food sources for wildlife such as deer and smaller mammals, and countless birds. Those plants that retain their berries or seeds through winter are especially important and will attract wildlife to the winter garden.

Combining native and exotic plants

Because this is a book about native plants, we have talked little about exotic species. Most of our gardens are filled with plants from different parts of the world, and you may be wondering if it is possible or appropriate to combine native plants with them. It definitely is.

This book is written for two types of native plant gardeners. The first is the gardener who has decided to devote the entire garden, or a large portion of it, to native plants. The second type of native plant gardener may not have enough space, or time, to recreate a natural plant community, but has particular favorites among the plants of the hills, forests, or fields nearby and wants to grow these in the landscape. This gardener may devote a small area to several native plant companions or may combine natives with exotic plants in a perennial flower border or shrub row, or at the house entry.

Both of these approaches are valid ways to landscape with native plants, and will allow you to bring the

Top: *A small New Orleans courtyard shows how natives and exotics can be combined to carry out a unified theme. Here native yucca and river birch combine with exotics that reflect the subtropical theme.*

Bottom: *Serviceberries (Amelanchior alnifolia) one of the many native berries that are edible, ripen in June and July. Birds like them too.*

unique beauties of native plants into your garden. However, certain mistakes can be made in combining native plants with exotic species, and these can make your work much more difficult, and prevent the native species from fitting in with the other plants or surviving in the garden at all. The following guidelines will help you avoid these mistakes.

First, decide how you want to use native plants in your garden. How much room will you devote to them? Do you want to grow a few favorite plants or a mixture of the plants of a particular native community? By deciding ahead of time exactly how you'll use native plants, you will avoid taking on too big a project and will be able to plan to meet the specific light, moisture, and soil needs of each native species you do plant.

Growing a few isolated native plants may be more difficult than maintaining a carefully planned arrangement of native plant companions. Growing the plants that are found together in nature helps to establish the proper habitat and microclimate for each species. This is one reason we've stressed the study of native plant communities in this book. If you do want to plant just a few wildflowers or native shrubs among your exotic plants, do your best to duplicate the soil and microclimate of their native communities. Plant them in landscape areas similar to their native habitats and provide shade when necessary by planting near buildings or tall plants, or by constructing a shade structure.

When combining native plants and exotics in the same garden area, be certain that all species have the same cultural needs. Many shrubs and wildflowers native to the West, for example, will not tolerate excessive summer water and will die if planted among frequently watered exotic shrubs.

Native plants often have specific soil needs, too: some wetland plants do best in a mixture of peat and sand, while many alpine species require a very open, gritty soil with rapid drainage. Some native species do best in conditions of low soil fertility. Learn about the needs of each species by studying its native habitat and community. Combine each native species with exotic plants that have similar needs.

Gravel makes a natural and practical walk through this woodland scene. The native azaleas and rhododendrons form walls of color along the path.

To give visual unity to the garden, combine native plants with exotic species of similar form, texture, and leaf size and color. Because plants evolve their physical characteristics partly in response to climate, you can often find exotic plants to match natives of your region among plants in other areas of the world with similar climates. For instance, many shrubs and trees of the Mediterranean region have the same evergreen habit and the small, hard, resinous leaves that characterize the native chaparral species of North America, because they also come from a region of mild winters and hot, dry summers. Similarly, good matches for many eastern woodland wildflowers and shrubs can be found in the plants of temperate Asia. These include many exotic species of rhododendron and other attractive flowering plants that look at home in a forest setting.

Planting overly vigorous or invasive exotic plants with your native species can create a number of problems. Some native species are not fast growers, and lack the vigor to compete with imported plants. Some exotic plants come from regions of the world where they are held in check by a rigorous climate or natural enemies; freed of these restraints, they can become pests in our gardens. Carefully study the exotic plant species you want to use, and learn about their size at maturity, rate of growth, and possible invasive qualities (such as the suckering roots of many bamboos). Avoid exotic species that have already become a nuisance in your area—plants once introduced into a few local gardens that now infest every pasture or patch of woodland for miles around.

Designing with other landscape materials

Plants, although the most important part of your garden, are not its sole content. You will probably combine plants with pavings, walls, paths, fences, and other structural elements.

When choosing materials to combine with your native plants, remember that those with an informal, natural look often blends best. Natural stone, unsurfaced boards or railroad ties, gravel and crushed rock from local sources, and even wood chips used for paths will imitate the soft shapes, textures, and flowing lines of the plants and plant groupings of your natural environment. If you can obtain most of the materials from local sources, they will blend best with the soils and plants of the region, and you will probably save money. In some cases, you may want to use more formal materials, such as concrete paving, crushed white dolomite rock, or surfaced and stained lumber, to contrast with the natural forms of the garden or blend your natural garden with more formal garden areas. Do this with caution, to avoid overpowering the subtle beauties of the native plants.

Pavings and walks

Informal materials for pavings and walks include many types of regional stone or brick products: adobe in the Southwest, flagstone in the East, and crushed stone from local quarries in many areas. Wood chips are useful for small forest paths, and may be obtained free or at minimal cost from your town park department or from a local tree service. More formal materials can be treated so that they blend with the colors of soil and plants. Concrete can be changed by earth-tone masonry dyes, and brick can be laid in an open pattern on sand, with small ground cover and herb plants planted between the bricks. Some paths can be created without added materials. For instance, regular mowing can define a meandering trail through a meadow or prairie.

Walls

Railroad ties and rough timbers have a rugged, natural appearance, and make durable walls. These walls, as well as others of board lumber or even brick and concrete, can be softened with shrubs placed along their base or cascading from above.

Stone

Rough stone is one of the most ancient and beautiful of materials for walls. Local stone is available in many parts of the country, deposited near

Slabs of salvaged concrete were laid to create these woodland stairs, with various "crack plants" giving them the romantic air of a ruin. Blooming plants are an oriental rhododendron *(right side)* and Japanese Menziesia purpurea *(upper left).*

the surface by the glaciers of the Ice Age or quarried from deep bedrock. Small and medium stones can be used for dry or mortared walls. Dry-laid walls can be built with small pockets of soil between the stones, and here you can grow small stonecrops, rock plants, succulents, and ground covers. If you build a wall with mortar, try to conceal the mortar joints so that you present a more natural appearance.

Another way to use stone in the natural landscape is to position large boulders in the planting areas. This is most effective when recreating a habitat in which such stones play a part. Use local stones if available but, whatever the source of stone, use just one type in the garden—rounded boulders from a particular locale, sharp rubble from a quarry, or whatever else you obtain. Position the stones in groups (the Japanese usually work with odd-numbered groups of one, three, or five stones), and bury each stone the way it was originally buried in nature.

Fencing

Simple materials for fencing include rough-milled board lumber, grape stakes, and split rails. If left unstained, these will weather to a soft brown or grey color. For a fence you can see through, build a standard framework of wood posts and stringers 5 or 6 feet high, and staple welded wire fencing to it. The wire will be less visible if you paint it black before installation. This is ideal to keep children or dogs in, or wild animals out, yet allows pleasant views of a surrounding natural area, stream, or woodland.

Water in the garden

Water adds great beauty to the natural garden. If you already have a stream, pond, or river on your property, you are fortunate. Arrange trees, shrubs, and flowers along its banks, let a garden path meander beside it, and plant special native species in the unique habitats created there.

Even if you don't have a stream or pond on your property, you may

Emphasize even the smallest trickle of water with plants of the water's edge, like ferns and saxifrages. Lure garden visitors across a stream with a path and a bridge, however small. This bit of a wood bridge fits the woodland habitat in which it was built so well that it looks almost as if it fell there by accident.

have a low area that collects drainage water during rains, or a drainage ditch running along your front road. Any such area can be shaped, widened, and dug out, and the soil amended and planted with the native plants of wet areas to provide a welcome variety in your garden.

If you are modifying an existing stream or pond on your site, observe similar water elements in nearby natural areas. Imitate their shape, the curve of their banks, and the nearby growth of herbaceous plants, shrubs, and trees, in your own design.

You can even imitate the form of a natural body of water or stream in a dry part of your garden, fashioning a dry stream course or pond hollow to suggest the presence of water, as some

Japanese gardens do. Place stones of varying size in the shape of a stream, to help create this illusion.

Preparing the landscape plans

Begin making your final landscape plans by referring back to your landscape analysis sketches or notes. These summed up your site analysis, and the activities and effects you want in your landscape. Look at the list of required activity areas for your site, which may include such different needs as a quiet outdoor sitting area, active game areas, and utility and work areas. Decide where each should be located. Try out different placements in a series of schematic diagrams, using a small circle or "bubble" to represent each activity

area. Do these drawings on tracing paper overlays of your base plan. If your garden already exists, and you are planning small uses of native plants with no major modifications, skip this design step and move on to prepare your planting plan.

Position the most important activities or areas first and then, as space remains, decide where to locate other use areas. Try a number of different layouts, matching the requirements of each activity with the site characteristics of different areas. For example, in a cool region you should locate an outdoor patio in a sunny spot. (In a hot region you might choose a cool side of the house.) Areas for active children's play should be dry and fairly level. A vegetable or cutting flower garden requires an area of deep soil and full sun. Areas used for outdoor entertaining are best located near the kitchen and living room. It is also possible to combine activities in some areas, such as using a paved area for both games and overflow parking.

Examine each layout to see that use areas are conveniently located, and that adjacent areas are compatible with each other (an example of incompatibility would be an outdoor entertainment area overlooking a food garden that will look unkempt in some seasons). Decide how to tie different parts of the landscape together on your schematic diagram, sketching in formal walks, informal paths, driveways, and other circulation routes. Examine the whole picture. Does the combined layout make sense and seem attractive?

Once you are satisfied with a schematic diagram of your site's use areas, begin to define each area more specifically. How large should it be? How much screening is needed between one area and another? What types of plants are needed in each area—where do you need a tall mass of dark evergreen trees, an umbrella of shade, a dense planting of medium or tall shrubs, or a carpet of native grasses or ground covers?

The site plan

Now draw your site plan. Trace your base plan onto graph or drafting paper. Trace all the data from the base plan, including the house and other structures, utility lines, and major existing landscape elements. Add the information from your final bubble diagram: the approximate layout of new or redesigned landscape areas, circulation routes, and major masses of plants.

If you are building new garden structures, adding large paved areas, or planning to modify topography or drainage patterns, note these changes on the site plan to keep the planting plan less cluttered. Find the sections in the last chapter that deal with your type of natural garden for specific suggestions in these areas. Your completed site plan guides you in the construction and preparation of your natural garden, and readies you to designate specific plantings that are recorded on the planting plan.

The planting plan

Begin your planting plan by referring first to the notes on the plant habitats of your site that are recorded in your landscape analysis drawings. Note different combinations of soil (type, texture, and available moisture), temperature, and light intensity. Summarize the plant habitats on an overlay of the base plan, identifying specific areas of wet, heavy, deep soils; shallow or rocky terrain; full sun; and pockets of shade. Note the plant types, such as tall trees, tall or low-growing shrubs, forbs, grasses, or ground covers, and heights needed for each type of planting. Write these next to the habitat notes on your overlay.

Now choose the native plants you'll use for each area. How you do this depends on how you are using native plants in your garden. If you are recreating native plant communities, consider the type of plants you need and the plant habitat that exists in each part of your site, and choose the appropriate native community. For example, if you need a screen of tall evergreen trees for a shallow, sandy soil on your site in the coastal Southeast, you could plant one or more of the pine species of the pine barrens which are found in this region, together with their natural companions of wire grass, turkey oak, and various forbs. On a deeper, more fertile soil, you could use the trees of the outer coastal plain forest, including southern magnolia, red bay, and live oak, with their associated small palms, evergreen shrubs, and ferns. If you lack the space to include many plants, you can represent a community by planting its dominant trees and a few characteristic theme plants, as discussed on pages 32-33.

If you are using native plants in a smaller area of your garden or combining individual native species with exotic plants in garden areas, the process is similar. Match the individual native species of your region to the type of plant you want in each area, and the habitat in that part of the garden.

To assist you in choosing native plants for your landscape, a number of plant lists are included in the final chapter. Look up the list of plants for your region of the country in the section dealing with the type of natural garden you wish to create; plants for forest, meadow, prairie, shrubland, seaside, desert, and alpine gardens are each discussed separately.

As you get an idea of the plants you want to use, visualize each in the garden. How will it look there? Will it blend or contrast attractively with the plants of nearby areas? How can you use the form, density, color, and texture of these plants together to emphasize what is important, what can frame views and unify the garden's design? Avoid the mistake of placing the native plants of two very different communities near each other, as this can confuse your design; instead, blend the plants of one community into those of the other by using plants that typically grow side by side in nature.

You can test your planting design ideas by drawing sketches, perspective views, and diagrams of the vertical structure of each planned landscape area. These drawings will be most helpful if you draw them to scale, as you probably did in your planting plan. Good scales to use are 1 inch = 4 feet and 1 inch = 8 feet. Draw the plants at their mature size (see the plant lists or other references for this information). In a scale of 1 inch = 8 feet (called 1/8 inch scale), for instance, a tree that reaches a mature height of about 30 feet and a spread of 50 feet would measure about 4 inches by 6 inches in your drawing. You can include in these drawings a part of your house or any other important structure, to get an idea of the relationship of the mature plants to the buildings as well as to each other. These drawings, perspectives, and other types of sketches can help you avoid making the common mistakes of choosing plants that will become too big for your garden or spacing the plants incorrectly when planting them as seedlings.

When you are satisfied with your plant selections, complete the planting plan. If your site plan is a simple and clear drawing and you are not planting a great many new plants in the landscape, you can combine the planting information with the site data on that sheet. If your planting project is large or complex, use a separate sheet. Trace onto the planting plan the elements of the basic site layout that circumscribes the garden areas: the house and other buildings, main paved areas, and paths. Then draw in the largest plants first (usually the trees) as circles on the plan. The center of the circle is where you will plant a young tree; the circle itself marks the expected spread of the branches at maturity. (In the example above, the tree with a mature spread of 50 feet would be drawn on a plan with a scale of 1 inch = 8 feet as a circle 6¼ inches in diameter. A shrub with a mature spread of 8 feet would be a circle of 1 inch diameter). After drawing in the trees, add the large shrubs, smaller shrubs, and forbs, grasses, and ground covers. These smallest plants will often be too small and numerous to draw individually, so show them as outlined areas, with a marginal note indicating the species and how far apart the individual plants are. Include also the major existing plants of the garden.

Note on the plan any instructions for soil preparation or special planting techniques to be used in different areas. In the margin or on a separate page, list the plants, giving the common and botanical name of each (you'll usually order them by botanical name), how many of each you need, and their source (whether you'll grow them from seed or cuttings, buy small seedlings from a nursery, or invest in large container-grown or field-dug plants). Also list the other materials you'll need and the amount of each, from soil amendments to paving materials to wood chips.

You will use the finished site plan and planting plan to install your landscape. The plans should contain all the information you need to build garden structures or paths, shape the land, prepare the soil, and plant.

Growing native plants

If you can't find the wildflowers you want in a nursery, there are several ways to raise your own. You can collect wild seed, make cuttings, or layer wild plants.

Interest in gardening with native plants has grown rapidly in recent years. Gardeners in the Midwest are designing and planting gardens of prairie grasses and forbs; the brilliant wildflowers of our native forests are finding homes in gardens from New England to the Pacific Northwest; and the unique shrubs, trees, and cacti of the deserts are increasingly popular in southwestern gardens.

Because this upsurge of interest is recent, the nursery trade in most areas has not yet caught up with it. Wholesale plant growers still produce only very limited numbers of native species, and most garden centers sell even fewer. The native plants of some regions are virtually unavailable in the trade. The result is that you may have trouble finding the native plants you want for your landscape.

If so, this chapter will be of help. It lists several mail-order and retail nurseries that sell seed and plants of native species. It also tells you how to gather seeds and root cuttings from native plants, and how to establish the new plants in the garden.

Sources of native seed and plants
You can buy native plants in several forms. The least expensive way is as seeds, which are then grown into seedlings in flats or pots, or sown

Tidy tips (Layia platyglossa) in a California coastal meadow are good candidates for seed collection.

directly outdoors on your site. Many of the sources listed below also sell young plants of native species and will ship these to you by mail. More expensive options are the larger plants sometimes available in containers, balled-and-burlapped, or bare-root. Usually, the larger the plants you buy, the more rapidly your garden will fill in and look established, but you may not be able to obtain all native species as large—or even small—plants; many can only be bought as seed.

Some nurseries raise most of their own plants from seed or cuttings; others sell plants they have collected in the wild. We recommend that you ask a nursery whether it does its own propagation and growing, and patronize those that do. There are two reasons for this. First, nurseries and individuals that collect wild plants have depleted some native species to near-extinction. Second, many native plants simply do not transplant well from their native habitat to a garden. If you buy collected plants and set them in the garden, they may only survive one or two years despite your best efforts. Nursery-grown plants usually adjust more readily.

When possible, buy your seed and plants from a local source. Choose the nurseries on the list that are located nearest to you, or find other sources in your area. Locally grown seed and plants have adapted to the particular climate and soils of your area, and will do better in your garden than seed or plants of the same species raised in a different area.

Collecting your own seed
The seed of many native plants can be harvested easily from mature plants growing in native communities in the wild or in the garden. The first step in collecting seed is to decide which of the native plants you want.

Mark a plant whose form you particularly like with a flag, so you can find it when the bloom is gone.

Sources of native plants and seeds

This list is partial at best. Many other nurseries and growers exist in each region of the country, and you can also obtain native seed and plants from botanical gardens and arboreta, native plant societies, wildflower preserves, and other gardeners. Catalog policies vary; contact the nursery for current policy and price.

Arthur Eames Allgrove
North Wilmington, MA 01887
Northeastern ferns and wildflowers, including orchids. Plants only.

Beersheba Wildflower Gardens
Stone Door Road
Beersheba Springs, TN 37305
Woodland wildflowers. Plants only.

Bernardo Beach Native Plant Farm
Star Route 7, Box 145
Veguita, NM 87062
Southwestern trees, shrubs and wildflowers. Plants only.

Blue Oak Nursery
2731 Mountain Oak Lane
Rescue, CA 95672
California trees, shrubs and wildflowers. Plants only.

Richard R. Clinebell
1874 Church Street
San Francisco, CA 94131
Northern Illinois prairie and woodland plants. Seeds only.

Cornflower Farms
Box 896
Elkgrove, CA 95624
California native plants.

Daystar
Litchfield-Hallowell Road
R.F.D. 2
Litchfield, ME 04350
Alpines and rock garden plants

Dry Country Plants
3904 Highway 70 East
Las Cruces, NM 88001
Southern New Mexico native plants specializing in flowering perennials.

Environmental Wildflowers
Box 5125
El Monte, CA 91734
California bulk wildflower seed, including mixes. Seeds only.

EST Wildflowers
Box 5125
El Monte, CA 91734
Bulk seeds, free catalog.

Fern Hill Farm
Route 3, Box 305
Greenville, AL 36037
Southern ferns and wildflowers. Plants and seeds.

Gardens of the Blue Ridge
Box 10
Pineola, NC 28662
Appalachian wildflowers, ferns and shrubs, including wetland plants.

Horizon Seeds, Inc.
Box 886, East Highway 60
Hereford, TX 79045
Native prairie grasses. Seeds only.

Horticultural Systems, Inc.
Box 70
Parrish, FL 33564
Southeastern beach and wetlands plants. Plants only.

Illini Gardens
Box 125
Oakford, IL 62673
Eastern woodland wildflowers. Plants only.

LaFayette Home Nursery, Inc.
Route 1, Box 1A
LaFayette, IL 61449
Native trees, shrubs, wildflowers, and prairie grasses. Plants and seeds.

Larner Seeds
Box 60143
Palo Alto, CA 94306
California and western plants. Seeds only.

Little Valley Farm
RR 1, Box 287
Richland Center, WI 53581
Prairie and woodland wildflowers and prairie grasses. Plants and seeds.

Mid-Atlantic Wildflowers
Star Route, Box 226
Gloucester Point, VA 23062

Midwest Wildflowers
Box 64
Rockton, IL 61072
Prairie and woodland wildflowers. Seeds only.

The Natural Garden
38 W 443 Highway 64
St. Charles, IL 60174
Northern Illinois prairie grasses and forbs, and woodland wildflowers.

Natural Habitat Nursery
4818 Terminal Road
McFarland, WI 53558
Prairie seeds of southern Wisconsin. Seeds only.

New Mexico Cactus Research
Box 787, Dept.102
Belen, NM 87002
Cactus and succulents. Seeds only.

Northplan Seed Producers
Box 9107
Moscow, ID 83843
Western trees, shrubs, wildflowers, and grasses. Seeds only.

Northwest Biological Enterprises
23351 S.W. Bosky Dell Lane
West Linn, OR 97068
Pacific Northwest trees, shrubs, wildflowers, and ferns. Plants only.

Panfield Nurseries, Inc.
322 Southdown Road
Huntington, NY 11743
Woodland wildflowers and ferns. Plants only.

The Theodore Payne Foundation
10459 Tuxford Street
Sun Valley, CA 91352
California trees, shrubs, and wildflowers. Seeds and plants.

Plants of the Southwest
1812 Second Street
Santa Fe, NM 87501
Southwestern trees, shrubs, and wildflowers. Plants and seeds.

Plants of the Wild
Box 866
Tekoa, WA 99033
Trees, shrubs, vines, and ground covers of the Pacific Northwest.

Prairie Moon Nursery
Route 3, Box 163
Winona, MN 55987
Seeds and plants.

Prairie Restorations, Inc.
Box 327
Princeton, MN 55371
Central Minnesota prairie grasses and wildflowers. Seeds and plants.

Prairie Ridge Nursery
RR 2, 9738 Overland Road
Mt. Horeb, WI 53572
Southwestern Wisconsin prairie grasses and wildflowers. Seeds and plants.

Prairie Seed Source
Box 83
North Lake, WI 53064
Southeastern Wisconsin prairie grasses and wildflowers. Seeds only.

Redwood City Seed Co.
Box 361
Redwood City, CA 94064
California plants. Seeds only.

Clyde Robbins Seed Co.
Box 2366
Castro Valley, CA 94546
California plants. Seeds only.

Sexton Nursery
23340 Doane Creek Road
Sheridan, OR 97378
Rock garden plants, including species native to the West.

The Shop in the Sierra
Box 1
Midpines, CA 95345
California trees, shrubs, and wildflowers. Plants only.

Siskiyou Rare Plant Nursery
2825 Cummings Road
Medford, OR 97501
Northwestern native wildflowers and ferns. Plants only.

Southwestern Native Seeds
Box 50503
Tucson, AZ 85703
Native plants of the American West and Mexico. Seeds only.

Sunlight Gardens, Inc.
Andrea Sessions
Route 3, Box 286 B
London, TN 37774

Drs. John & Connie Taylor
Goldenrod Hollow
Route 1, Box 157
Durant, OK 74701

Wapumne Native Plant Nursery Co.
8305 Cedar Crest Way
Sacramento, CA 95826
California plants. Plants only.

Wildlife Nurseries
Box 2724
Oshkosh, WI 54901
Wetland plants (mostly native to upper Mississippi River drainage, and emphasizing species that attract waterfowl).

Windrift Prairie Shop and Nursery
R.D. 2
Oregon, IL 61061
Northern Illinois prairie grasses and wildflowers. Seeds and plants.

Woodlanders, Inc.
1128 Colleton Avenue
Aiken, SC 29801
Plants of the southern Piedmont and coastal plain. Plants only.

Yerba Buena Nursery
19500 Skyline Boulevard
Woodside, CA 94062
California plants, including ferns. Plants only.

Return to your marked field when some seedheads have formed to collect a supply of seed. Be sure to bring paper bags and label them carefully. Never take more than you can use, so the native stand can reproduce itself for others to enjoy.

Use this book and other native plant references for your region to choose the plants for your garden, to decide which you will propagate from seed, and to learn how to identify these plants in nature. The identification keys in many native plant manuals and regional *floras* (plant identification handbooks) will help you in this. Study plants in nature while they are in bloom; they are easily identified then, and you can see them at their best. Place a small stake or other marker next to each plant from which you want seed, because they will look different and may be harder to identify when their bloom is past and they are covered with seed capsules.

Return to collect the seed when it is mature. This will usually happen between August and November, depending on the species and the region of the country. As a general rule, mature seed on plants that produce a dry seed is dark and dry; plants that produce seed within a fleshy fruit or berry are usually ready for collection when the berries are most brightly colored. The best time to collect the seed is just before the plant would naturally disperse it from a shattering seed capsule or in a fruit consumed by birds or animals.

Gather the seed in small paper bags (it may mold or rot in plastic), and label each with the plant species and the date and place of collection. You can shake seed into a plastic pail or onto a tarp or, if necessary, snip off the entire seed head. In either case, take no seed that you don't plan to propagate and take only a small proportion of the seed from any one stand of plants, leaving the natural area undisturbed.

Clean seed from dry seed heads, pods, and capsules by leaving it in a paper bag for several days to finish drying. Then crush the seed structure between your hands or rub it back and forth over a fine-mesh screen that allows the seeds to fall through. Remove light chaff from heavy seeds by spreading them on a tray and gently blowing away the chaff.

Clean seed in a fleshy or pulpy fruit by macerating the fruit in a sieve and placing the pulp in a jar with water to float off the lighter pulp and nonviable seeds. Viable seed is heavier than water and will sink. Pour off the pulp and water, then dry the seed on newspaper or towels.

Collect and clean seed from native plants in your garden in the same way. You can also simplify collection and get cleaner seed by wrapping small paper bags tied with string around the seed heads and waiting for the plant to naturally ripen and disperse the seed into the bag.

After cleaning the seed, the easiest way to plant it is to follow nature's example: in the fall, sow it outdoors where you want it to grow. If you do this, see the following section on direct seeding in the garden. However, you may choose not to sow the seed immediately after cleaning. It may be scarce, or it may be dormant when collected and will not immediately germinate.

Growing native plants from seed

The least expensive and easiest way to grow native plants is from seed. It can also be very satisfying. In addition, many of the finest native species can only be obtained in seed form. Even the seed of some native species is not commercially available; in this case, you can have these plants in your garden by collecting the seed in nature. These are the advantages of raising plants from seed. The main disadvantage is that it can be a slow process: some species will take several years to attain sufficient size for garden transplanting.

The most common types of native plants grown from seed are annual and perennial wildflowers and grasses. Some woody shrubs can also be raised easily from seed.

Although nature will slowly overcome the dormancy of seeds that have been scattered in a prepared garden area, you can do it much more efficiently, germinate a greater number of seeds, and be better able to nurse those species that need several seasons to attain transplanting size, if you sow the seeds in flats or pots.

Seed storage and dormancy

Because brand new, tiny seedlings do not easily survive harsh winter conditions, plants in cold climates have evolved the mechanism of dormancy, which prevents seed from sprouting immediately after it is dispersed in late summer. Seeds from such climates usually require a cold period to fully ripen, and then germinate in the succeeding warm season. Many woody native plants, grasses, and forbs have seeds of this type, and their dormancy can be overcome simply by the process of *stratification*, which is the storage of seed in a moist planting medium for several months at cold temperatures. Seeds that are moist when mature usually require stratification. Place these seeds in polyethylene plastic bags in moist horticultural-grade vermiculite, which is available at most garden centers. Store the bags of seed at temperatures between 32°F and 41°F for about three months. This is most easily done in a refrigerator or unheated room. Seed can also be stratified in outdoor flats that are set into moist soil, gravel, or shavings, and covered with glass or plastic sheeting to keep out rodents and hard rain. In climates where the ground freezes, bury the seeds below the frost line.

Seeds that are dry when mature can usually be kept through the winter in dry storage, in airtight plastic bags in a refrigerator or other cold spot. Label each seed lot carefully so you'll know what you have when spring comes.

Some seeds have a more complicated dormancy, evolved to meet the rigors of drought and unfavorable growing conditions in their environment. Most common are several types of seed-coat dormancy. Some seeds have a hard seed coat, which keeps water from being absorbed by the seed, and some have a seed coat that contains chemical germination inhibitors, which must be leached out. Processes that are designed to break seed dormancy are called *scarification*. Two types of scarification are used to prepare these seeds for germination.

Some seeds are best scarified by a hot water treatment. Pour water of about 190°F (just below boiling) over the seeds. Use a volume of water 4 or 5 times that of the seeds, and let it stand overnight to cool. Sow the seeds before they dry. Seeds with a hard seed coat can also be scarified by tumbling with moist sand in a motorized rock polisher, or by shaking them in a coffee can lined with sharp sandpaper. The object is to wear away some of the seed coat but not to damage the seed itself. Large seeds can be nicked with the edge of a triangular file.

Sowing and germination

After scarification or stratification, sow treated seeds in flats or pots, several seeds to a pot. Many different mixes are used for different native species; a good all-purpose one is 1 part good garden loam to 1 part sand to 1 part moistened peat. Because some seedlings can be killed by soil-borne diseases, you may wish to buy a sterilized potting mix or sow the seeds in vermiculite. Moisten the planting medium before sowing and allow it to drain. Plant the seeds in rows and cover them with vermiculite or peat moss to a depth of about twice their thickness. Very small seeds can be mixed with an equal volume of sand to avoid overseeding. Cover the flat or pot with a clear plastic bag or place it in a cold frame covered with plastic or glass. Keep the soil moist by soaking from below or misting, and remove the plastic as the seedlings appear.

As soon as the seedlings are large enough to handle, transplant them into potting mix in larger flats or in

Wildflower seed mixes

One popular way to buy native plants is as wildflower seed mixes. Many nurseries and seed companies offer these, some even selling them nationwide through their own catalogs, magazine advertisements, and mail-order houses.

Several types of wildflower mixes are available. Local seed mixtures are usually sold by small regional native plant nurseries, and are selections of native plant seed from their own collecting expeditions. Local seed mixes are collected in and blended for a very specific geographic area and type of habitat—an example might be a mix of prairie grasses and forbs for the northern Midwest.

If you can obtain a local seed mix for your area, it should give you a successful garden of the wildflowers native to the area. Because the seed is collected locally, it is from plants that are adapted to the climate, soils, and other conditions of the area, and it should thrive in your garden and represent the native plants and communities of your region. However, local seed mixtures are not available in many areas; if you can't find one blended for your locale, your alternatives are to buy a local seed mix for an area similar to your own or to get a regional or national wildflower mix.

Regional wildflower mixes are selections of seeds from many native species of a wide geographic region, such as the western United States. (Other regional mixtures are available for the central prairies, Eastern states, deserts, and mountain regions.) These mixes are blended to include seeds of some species that are native to each of the major habitats of the region, so that a typical mix may contain some species that thrive on wet soil, others that prefer dry, stony locations, and still more that require a rich woodland habitat. The idea behind this type of seed mix is that wherever it is sown, some of the species will find it favorable, and grow and flower, while those not adapted will simply not survive.

Regional seed mixtures can be successful in bringing the beauty of wildflowers to your garden. When selecting a regional mix, choose the blend that seems most specific to your area (for instance, a desert mix for a very hot, dry region, or a mountain mix for higher elevations) and buy it from the closest source possible to ensure some bred-in tolerance of your climate and soils. Note also the list of the species included in the mix; many seed companies include European native wildflowers (such as Shirley poppy and chicory) with true American natives. There is nothing wrong with planting these species, and many of them are very beautiful.

However, if you wish to concentrate on American native plants, you may want to avoid such mixtures. If the mixture you choose does include exotic wildflowers, be certain before sowing that none of the imported species will escape and become a garden pest in your area.

The third type of wildflower seed mix is the "national wildflower mix" now offered by several seed companies. These are blends of very hardy species from a wide variety of habitats all across this continent, and are put together on the same theory as regional mixtures: where one species won't grow, several others in the mix will, so that anyone almost anywhere in the country can grow flowers from the mixture.

National seed mixtures usually include still more exotic wildflowers than regional mixes, and because the seed may be from sources anywhere in the world, it may be less adapted to conditions in your region. Such a mix will be less predictable than either a local or a regional wildflower seed mix—it may grow and bloom beautifully or it may never really become established. What frequently happens is that plants from the seed mix grow into a beautiful tapestry of wildflowers the first year, but only one or two species reappear the second and subsequent years.

plastic or peat pots 2 or 3 inches in diameter. You can also plant them in well-worked, fine-textured nursery beds. Lift each seedling carefully from the flat with a wooden label or popsicle stick; avoid touching the stem or roots. If the seedling is a tree that forms a long tap root, pinch the tip off the root now. This will prevent the roots from coiling in the bottom of the pot later. Set the seedling carefully into the new soil and water it well.

By the time the seedling has reached this stage, it is probably fall. You will want to overwinter most seedlings in a cold frame for spring planting, or simply pull mulch around the pots or flats in milder climates. Fertilize them with a diluted liquid plant food for several weeks after transplanting. Check them periodically during the winter and protect them from burrowing animals or severe weather. Some species are especially slow-growing from seed, and may need several years in pots before being planted in the garden.

Direct sowing in the garden

The easiest way to handle seed is to sow it directly in the garden. This is also the best strategy if you are unsure of the type of dormancy and the required treatments for germination, because its dormancy will eventually be overcome by natural processes in the garden.

Large, tough seeds with simple dormancy mechanisms respond happily to direct sowing, and sprout during the following spring. Direct sowing may not break the dormancy of other species quickly, however, and plants may straggle up slowly over 2, 3, or even 10 years. The seedlings of still other species are slow-growing, and may be buried by winter rains and mud or easily choked by weeds if the ground is not clean.

Top: *Plastic or wooden label sticks and a waterproof marking pen are indispensable in remembering what seeds you planted.*

Center: *Hold seedlings by the leaves and gently work the roots free.*

Bottom: *Pot in individual containers of increasing size, then plant out. You can avoid losses due to pests by setting out well-established seedlings.*

Despite these drawbacks, direct seeding is an effective way of propagating many native species in the landscape and is the only economical way to plant large areas of some natural landscapes.

Before sowing, eliminate the weeds in the area. Clean the ground, till it, and keep it moist for a few weeks to germinate any weed seeds in the soil. Kill these seedlings with shallow cultivation or an herbicide. Be especially careful to eradicate those difficult species that could ruin your natural garden later—such weeds as Bermuda grass, reed canary grass, and field bindweed. Kill these weeds with a systemic herbicide. Make sure they are completely eradicated before planting.

To sow your natural garden, first gather the appropriate amount of seed for your site. This is dependent on the species, the quality of your site, and how much seed you expect to lose to birds, poor germination, and other factors. Stratify the seed, and scarify it if required. Amend the soil or adjust its pH with additions of lime or sulfur if that is needed in your area. Sow the seed in fall, right after you collect or purchase it. Sow seed by broadcasting by hand or with a broadcast seeder. Use half the seed mixture on the first pass over the area, then go back over the entire area with the second half. This insures that you won't run out of seed, and that the ground will be covered evenly. Water the seeds with a fine fan-spray type of nozzle; this will settle them slightly into the earth. You can also rake them into the soil lightly, or cover them with about ⅛ inch of good soil.

If rains do not come right away, keep them watered regularly, never allowing the ground to dry out between waterings. In mild climates, several weeks will be enough to bring up the first seedlings, with more following gradually according to their dormancy and germination times. In colder climates, you'll begin to see germination in spring, and this will continue for several years. The seedlings of some native plants, especially those of difficult climates such as the plains and prairies, may show little growth above ground for the first few seasons, while they are busily building their tremendous root systems. In time, the tops will also begin to grow vigorously. Be patient and keep the area weeded.

Other propagation methods

Besides starting plants from seeds, several other methods can be used to begin new plants. All these other methods are *vegetative*, which means that the new plants will be genetically identical to their parents. Seedlings are a mix of the characteristics of both of their parents, but vegetatively propagated plants have only one parent. If you collect cuttings from a bushier-than-normal lupine, the offspring will be bushier than normal,

This well-rooted cutting is ready for hardening off, which gradually adjusts the new plant to an unprotected growing site.

too. Pay attention not only to the species that you collect from, but also to the specimen's individual characteristics.

Cuttings

Small stems or branches removed from most plants can be encouraged to grow roots and leaves and to form a new plant. These small pieces of larger plants are called *cuttings*, and are an easy way to propagate many herbaceous and woody native species.

Cuttings can be taken from plants in your garden or in a friend's, or from plants in the wild. If you take cuttings from wild plants, observe the same courtesies mentioned above for gathering seed: take only what you need, remove no more than a few stems from a plant that has many, and leave the area undisturbed by your presence. You will probably need a permit to make cuttings in parks and national forests.

Softwood cuttings

From most plants, you will take *softwood* cuttings, which are green, pliant wood with the leaves still attached.

Redwood cuttings form a miniature forest on this commercial greenhouse tabletop.

Because the cuttings will be actively metabolizing even before they form new roots, they are prone to drying out and wilting throughout the rooting process. Prevent this, or they will not root. Make softwood cuttings from mid-spring to early summer, before the plants set buds for the winter. The best time to collect cuttings for most species is just as the leaves expand fully in the spring. Remove small branches and wrap them in damp cloth or polyethylene to prevent wilting on the way home.

Prepare the cuttings promptly by pulling small side branches (each 3 to 5 inches long with several leaves attached) from the larger branches. Remove the lowest leaves from each cutting, and dip the base in a commercially available rooting hormone. Have ready a deep box or flat, or small pots, about half-full of a mixture of 5 parts perlite and one part peat moss. Perlite is a processed rock product that is available at nurseries. Wet the medium, then let it drain. Punch holes several inches apart in the planting medium and insert the cuttings, firming the medium around each. Water the box or pot with a fine spray of water, and place it within a small frame built of wire and covered with plastic in the greenhouse or glass-covered cold frame, or in a shady spot outdoors if your climate is mild. Pull soil around the bottom of the plastic to make a tight seal. Remove the plastic and mist or water the soil as often as necessary to keep the "tent" humidity very high.

Once the roots are 1 to 2 inches long, normally about 6 weeks after cutting, the new plants can be gradually moved to the garden. It's best to make the transition slowly from the carefully controlled temperatures and humidity to the garden, first moving the cuttings to a cold frame or shaded area for several weeks, then exposing them to more sun each day until they can tolerate it without wilting. This process is called *hardening off*. When the cuttings are acclimated to the outdoors, transplant them carefully into small containers for further growth, or into the garden.

Hardwood cuttings

These cuttings are collected from some deciduous trees and shrubs and from some conifers. You will make hardwood cuttings in fall or winter

Ribes speciosum is among the plants that can be propagated by layering. A branch held under the soil surface by a forked stick will root, producing a detachable plant. This is a slow process, however, requiring at least one and maybe two seasons.

when the plant is dormant. Hardwood cuttings differ from softwood cuttings in several ways. They are woody rather than green and pliant, usually have no leaves attached, and have buds already formed for next spring's growth. They are treated somewhat differently, too. Select twigs of the previous season's growth and cut to a length of 6 to 8 inches. Cut the bottom end at a slant and the top end square so you can tell which is which. Dip the bottom end into rooting hormone, bundle the cuttings with string, and place them in a moist medium of sand or wood shavings. Pack them in boxes that are set a little way into the ground in a cool place outdoors. Store them here through the winter, keeping them moist and safe from freezing. In colder climates, store them indoors in an unheated garage or basement. In early spring, open the bundles and set each cutting upright into a pot of a good rooting mix (5:1 perlite:peat is good for this, too), or into its permanent spot in the garden. The cuttings will form roots first, then shoots. Be patient: some hardwood cuttings take up to two years to be ready for transplanting into the garden.

Layering

You can root cuttings without removing them from the parent plant by a method called *layering*. This works

best with plants that have flexible stems that can be bent to the ground, including many trailing shrubs such as bearberry and box huckleberry.

Layering, like other forms of cuttings and division, allows you to grow a new plant with characteristics identical to its parent, so choose the parent plant carefully.

Layering is usually done in early spring, before growth begins. Young branches formed during the previous year's growth will root most easily. When you find the plant you want to reproduce, dig a shallow pit or trench near it, and pull the stem (still attached to the plant) into the trench. Hold the middle of the stem down in the trench with a bent wire or notched peg, and cover it with soil. If the soil around the plant is stiff and heavy, fill the trench with a lighter soil mix. Bend the outer end of the stem upward from the trench, and attach it in a nearly vertical position to a stake. Cutting a small notch or cracking the stem slightly on its lower side where it bends upward from the trench will help the rooting process. The staked, vertical stem will be your new plant.

In most cases, one season's growth will be adequate to form roots on the underground portion of the upright stem, though it will form a stronger root system if it is not dug until the second year. Remove it in early

Clumping perennials, like this sisyrinchium, *may become overcrowded and die out in the center if not divided. Divide them every few years to keep them growing actively and to help them spread faster.*

spring by carefully severing it from the parent plant and lifting it from the soil, then plant it promptly in a nursery bed or in its garden location.

Dividing herbaceous perennials

Many native plants, especially clump-forming herbaceous plants such as aster and wild ginger, can be divided after several years' growth. Because divisions are mature plants with full root systems, they establish and fill in rapidly in the garden.

Divide plants early in spring before growth begins, or in late summer or fall, after they have finished blooming. Cut back aboveground stems to a few inches' height, pry the mass gently out of the ground with a spade, grasp the short stems, and pull the plants apart. Simply pulling the clumps apart works for most species; with some, you'll need to cut them apart with a sharp knife. Each division must have roots and a bud. Plant it promptly in prepared soil in its permanent garden position. Some native plants can be divided every few years. Others form tough, stringy clumps that can only be divided when young.

Bulbs

A few native plants grow from a bulb or similar underground storage root. If they are content where placed in the garden, the bulbs will multiply underground, and the new bulbs can be dug and replanted elsewhere. With most species, this is done in late summer or fall when the foliage has turned yellow and withered.

Root divisions

Those plants, such as sumac, that form spreading clumps and many upright suckers, can be propagated from pieces of their spreading, horizontal roots. Look for pencil-thick roots in early spring, before the plants begin active growth. Cut pieces 2 to 6 inches long, noting which end of the piece was nearer the center of the plant. Dip this end in rooting hormone. Stratify the pieces in bundles for several weeks in a cool, moist medium (see the method given for hardwood cuttings). Then plant, with the cutting set vertically so that the end that was nearest the center of the plant is on top.

Removing native plants from the wild

This method of obtaining native plants for your garden is rarely appropriate. In many states, it is illegal to collect wild plants. Although often done in the past by avid native plant gardeners, collecting plants in the wild has led some species almost to extinction. It is also difficult to move plants from their natural habitat to the garden successfully, and few survive for more than a season or two. And it is no longer necessary to find many native species in this way because they are now being grown in the nursery trade. Those species still unavailable from commercial sources can usually be propagated from seed or cuttings obtained in the wild or from other gardeners.

Probably the only acceptable occasion for digging plants from the wild is when the area is about to be leveled and developed. If you can, prepare your garden areas for the wild plants before you dig them, learning everything possible of their habitat requirements and provide soil pH, moisture, and light intensity to match their natural environment. Be sure to obtain permission from the landowner in advance. Arrive with a shovel, twine, pails, and plastic bags or tarps, depending on the size of the plants. Remove the plants by digging carefully around each root ball, trying not to sever any roots, and gradually digging beneath the plant and lifting it from the earth. Take as large a root ball as possible and wrap it securely to avoid damage on the trip home. On returning home, immediately set the plants in their permanent location. If you can't plant them immediately, set them all in a trench in a well-worked bed or pile of good soil, pull the soil over the root balls, and water them thoroughly. Move these plants as soon as possible to their permanent garden positions.

Establishing native plants in the garden

Study, proper preparation, and a watchful eye are all important in making your new plants comfortable in the garden. Before planting, study each species to learn its needs and the habitat conditions under which it thrives. Design your garden to place each species in appropriate soil, moisture, and light conditions, and with the other plants of its native community whenever possible. Remove actively growing weeds and germinate weed seeds in the soil so that they can be killed. Plant new seedlings and young plants during the cool seasons of spring and fall, especially in regions where summers are dry. Keep them moist at all times until they are actively growing, and provide extra shade, if it is needed, with temporary shade structures of latticework or burlap hung between poles. Fertilize young seedlings with a diluted solution of a balanced liquid fertilizer. Protect them with mulch during the first few winters.

Some native plants are better added during the second, third, or even fifth year, once the soils are fertile and mellow and the major plants of the garden have established a benign microclimate. Examples of these tender natives are some spring wildflowers of the eastern forests, certain of the small grasses and forbs of the prairie, and some of the most handsome shrubs of the western chaparral community. Begin to add these plants to the new landscape after several seasons of growth, planting them in carefully prepared pockets of soil, and watch them carefully during the first few seasons.

Have patience with your native plant garden. It may be several years before it feels like more than just a collection of plants. You will fail with some plants, succeed with others. Through it all you'll continue learning about the native plants of your region, and you'll watch your garden grow in beauty.

A home nursery

If you will be establishing a large native plant garden and propagating many plants from seed or cuttings, consider setting aside a part of your yard as a nursery area. You might include here a cold frame, several propagating beds, and perhaps a small greenhouse.

A cold frame is a large, bottomless wooden box, set on the ground, with a sloping, tight-fitting roof of transparent material. It is usually covered by a window sash or plastic-covered wood frame, and is oriented so that the roof faces south. Its only heat is provided by the sun during the day, and retained by the soil and the snug cover at night. Good cold frame sizes are 2 by 4 feet or 3 by 6 feet.

Use your cold frame for rooting cuttings or starting seed during spring, summer, or fall, or for hardening off rooted cuttings or seedlings being readied for the garden. Keep the cover closed to maintain high humidity when the plants are first set in the frame, then gradually open it for longer periods each day to accustom the plants to lower humidity.

Summer temperatures can become quite high in a cold frame. Place a piece of latticework or shade cloth made to fit over the glass to provide extra shade at these times. Protect plants from freezing temperatures by piling straw or sawdust around the frame or installing a heating cable beneath the soil inside it.

Complete directions for building your own cold frame are given in Ortho's book *How to Build and Use Greenhouses.*

The other important part of your

A cold frame allows you to moderate temperature for tender young seedlings. This simple design was built of plywood and reused windows.

home nursery is a propagating bed. This is an outdoor bed of well-worked garden loam, enriched with leaf mold or compost and screened to remove rocks. One or two beds 5 feet by 10 feet will be plenty for most gardens. You can sow the seeds of some native species directly in this bed (those that aren't quite hardy enough for direct sowing in the garden) and tend them carefully until they are ready for transplanting. You can also move young seedlings into this bed when they outgrow their flats.

An alternate type of propagating bed is simply a flat area covered with a shallow layer of gravel for drainage, in which you raise young seedlings or rooted cuttings in small containers.

Protect the plants in either type of bed from winter weather by building a wood frame a few inches above the bed and covering it with plastic sheeting. Extend the plastic to the ground and pull a mulch of shavings or straw up around the base of it for insulation. In mild climates, a deep mulch around the containers and the perimeter of the bed may be enough.

You may also want to include in your nursery area a small greenhouse. Here you can start seeds or root cuttings all year, and carefully control temperature and humidity for optimal growth of the young plants. Many small prefabricated greenhouses are available, or build your own, following instructions in Ortho's book *How to Build and Use Greenhouses,* or other references.

Native plant gardens

Specific details about the planting and care of different types of natural gardens, from northern forests to southern deserts.

I n this chapter are the instructions for building, planting, and maintaining your native plant garden. In previous chapters you have discovered the native plants of your region, assessed your site habitats and your landscape needs, and designed your garden. Now it's time to put the garden in, following the instructions below.

The chapter is organized into sections corresponding to the main types of native plant gardens: forest gardens, meadows, prairie gardens, chaparral, desert gardens, alpine gardens, seaside gardens, subtropical gardens, and water gardens. Read those sections that correspond to the native vegetation communities of your area and to your landscape plans. If your garden will be composed primarily of trees planted close together, with an understory of shrubs and shade-loving wildflowers, read the section on forest gardens. If you live in a desert region and will be planting the trees, shrubs, and annual wildflowers native to this environment, see the section on desert gardens. Each section covers the most important elements to be considered in designing the garden, preparing the soil, planting and sowing, and maintaining the garden.

If you have a large garden, you may be combining several types of native vegetation in imitation of the natural landscape. Perhaps you've designed a forest garden with a large

Red Indian paintbrush and bluebonnets are bright representatives of our floral national heritage.

wildflower meadow at its center, or a garden of chaparral shrubs that includes groves of woodland trees and a rock garden. In these cases, read the sections of text that describe each type of garden you'll have. Blend the different plant communities carefully; remember that two plant communities in nature do not simply meet at a dividing line, but blend over a large or small area in which characteristics and plants of both communities are found. In your garden, blend adjacent types of native plantings by using those species that typically grow at the edge between the communities in nature, and blend the physical appearance of the plantings as well, so that the forest trees gradually thin out approaching the meadow, and the seaside dune grasses gradually merge with the shrubs and trees on their landward side. In situations where the native plant garden adjoins a more formal garden, some type of blending is also important.

This is a small book on a large subject. For this reason, the information given in these sections is general in nature; the specifics of native soil types, exact sowing dates, and other details will differ in each locale.

Each section includes a list of plants suitable for that type of garden. Since hundreds or thousands of plants can be used for most of these gardens, the lists are partial. We chose plants that were typical of the plant community, that could be successfully grown in a home garden, and that were available in nurseries or from seed houses.

Use the lists in each section to select plants for the framework of your garden. If you want to explore the native plants of your region more thoroughly, you will find a brief bibliography in each section. The books listed usually describe the plants of their region in more detail than we have room for here.

In a desert garden, create an oasis of plants with high water needs near the house. Bluebonnets highlight an oasis bed of perennials in this Austin, Texas, landscape.

Rich tapestries like this Canadian woodland stream planting can be created gradually. Begin with the trees and shrubs, and gradually add the fine details. The pink blooming plant in the photo's center is showy lady's slipper.

In addition to these resources, your local cooperative extension office can offer advice on many aspects of gardening in your area, and may have many useful publications, including lists of local native plants.

Forest gardens

The native forests of North America are home to many beautiful evergreen and deciduous trees, a host of flowering shrubs, and hundreds of spring wildflowers. If you live in a forested region (or an area that was forested in the past), you can bring these beautiful native plants into your garden, using the native forest to inspire your design.

More has been written about this type of native plant garden than any other. It is sometimes called a woodland, shade, or wild garden. It can take the form of a dense, dark forest with very little growth beneath the trees (not the most interesting kind of garden) or, by spacing the trees more widely apart, a woodland. In a woodland, the tree canopies don't quite touch, and there is naturally room and light enough beneath the dominant trees for many understory trees and shrubs, and a rich ground cover of flowers, ferns, and mosses.

In this section, we'll talk about gardens based on the eastern and southeastern forests, the montane forests of the Rocky Mountain and the Sierra-Cascade ranges, and the Pacific coastal forest. Suggestions for gardens patterned after the woodland plant communities of the Western United States—the pinyon-juniper woodland of the Southwest and the live oak woodland of California—are included in the section on shrubland gardens, on page 69.

Design

Begin your garden by studying native forests in your area and comparing the conditions of light, soil, and moisture to the habitats in your garden. Look at the vertical layers and horizontal patterns of trees and shrubs in the forest, and note the most common plant associations in the community.

Now choose the plants you'll use, selecting the best native forest species for your garden according to your landscape needs and the plant habitats of your site. Choose a variety of plants to imitate the diversity of a real forest, but select your favorite forest trees, shrubs, and ground covers as the theme plants, to be repeated throughout the garden. Lay out the plants according to their habitat preferences and landscape functions, bringing together those with similar requirements. A well-selected list of forest plants will provide garden interest all year, from early spring wildflowers through azaleas and viburnums, and to the bare branches and bright berries of winter.

If your lot has an established grove of trees, you may want to remove a few of them to let in more light, pruning out dead branches and shaping the trees that remain. Your landscape plan in this case can simply show where you'll have masses of plantings beneath the trees, the arrangement of the garden areas, and the layout of paths. Add excitement to the design by carefully screening views and providing small "surprise" plantings along the paths.

You can also start a forest garden beneath just a few trees or even on bare ground. This will require several years of patience and work. Begin with a few tough, pioneer trees (those that first colonize open areas in your region, such as white birch and aspen in the North, and certain pines in the South) and hardy shrubs, planting them in pockets of improved soil. Follow the first plantings with the permanent trees you want as your garden's backbone, and gradually add tender shrubs and small flowering plants as the soil and micro-climate improve over several years. Your landscape plans will show the layout of the garden and the succession of plantings you'll make.

Give each plant plenty of room to attain its mature size. Design the edges of the forest to blend with the surrounding landscape. If your garden is large enough, include one of the plant communities typically found near forests: a meadow, alpine plants in a rock garden, or a prairie.

Soil preparation

If you are beginning a forest garden on bare ground, you can either use a small tractor or work by hand to shape the terrain into pleasing valleys, slopes, or hollows. This also creates varied plant habitats, with differing conditions of sun, shade, moisture, and soil depth. If you are making a garden under large trees, don't attempt to change the grade; trees are very sensitive to the depth of soil on their roots, and even a change of a few inches can harm them.

Kill perennial weeds that resprout from their roots, such as bamboo grass, Bermuda grass, and others. Treat them with a non-residual, systemic herbicide, such as glyphosate.

Now begin soil improvement. The soil is the heart of any garden, but it's especially important in a forest garden, where humus levels must be very high, and acidity and soil texture must be suitable for the particular plants you're growing. Some forest plants are tolerant of variations in soil fertility and acidity but many are not, and you'll need to meet their specific needs. Most forest plants need an acid soil and very quick drainage.

You can begin soil improvement for a forest garden by reclaiming and planting small areas, adding to your garden a bit at a time, or do the entire garden at once. One of the best strategies for small-area improvement is to dig up and amend small pockets of soil throughout the garden for individual trees, shrubs, and wildflowers. Decide where the major plants of the garden should be placed—it's very important to get major trees growing early—and improve these areas. Then plant with fertile, rich soil from established parts of the garden or with one of the soil mixes recommended below. You can accompany this spot planting with large-scale soil improvement in the rest of the garden by adding organic material as a mulch. If you are planting under existing trees, don't disturb the soil any more than necessary; plant in pockets and improve the rest of the garden with mulches.

Most forest plants prefer acidic soil. Some grow best in a mildly acidic, nearly neutral soil, and others in highly acidic soil. Acidity is measured on the pH scale. Acid garden soil typically ranges from a pH of 4.0 (very acidic) to 6.0 or 6.5 (near the neutral point of 7.0). A higher pH than 7.0 indicates soil with an alkaline reaction (common in dry areas of the West, but infrequent in forested areas). When improving pockets of soil for specific forest plants, learn the acidity preferences of each species (see references at the end of this section), and plant those with similar needs together. Test the pH of your soil with a simple soil test kit purchased at a nursery, or send samples to a soils lab (ask your cooperative extension service for a list of recommended labs). After amending the soil and planting, test pH annually in different garden areas.

To make a pocket planting mix for forest plants preferring slightly acidic-to-neutral soil, mix 2 parts good garden loam to 1 part coarse sand and 1 part leaf mold from maples, birches, or other soft-leaved plants (not oaks). For plants preferring more acidity, use sand and loam mixed with oak leaf mold. For those few plants preferring highly acidic

Flowers of the forest floor make a ground cover for this northeastern deciduous forest garden. They include Trillium *(lower right),* cranebill *(lower left),* pink phlox *(in middle distance) and white* Tiarella *(in background).*

conditions, mix equal parts of sandy loam soil, sand, and sphagnum peat.

If there are many weed seeds in the soil, keep the ground moist for a few weeks to germinate them. As they germinate, kill the seedlings with an herbicide or a shallow cultivation.

Garden construction

Create natural curves when laying out a forest garden by arranging the paths, plantings, and water elements to imitate natural lines. Where the forest garden approaches the house or meets a more formal garden, use more concentrated and distinct flower and shrub displays, and such formal elements as low, clipped hedges and brick or flagstone pavings to blend the two styles.

Paths are essential in the forest garden because many forest plants will not grow well in soil compacted by foot traffic.

Construction materials include locally quarried stone for walls and walks, wood chips and natural stepping stones for forest trails, and large

boulders. Position large stones or boulders so that stone and plant complement each other. Bury the rocks slightly to give them a stable and natural appearance. If the rock is aged or moss-covered, bury the same side as in its original location.

Certain water elements are natural in a forest garden: acid bogs are part of both Northern and Southeastern forest landscapes; a stream is a natural addition to any forest; and a small forest pool can support water-loving shrubs and perennial flowers.

Planting

The best planting times for most forest gardens are from early spring to mid-spring and fall. If transplanting, move the plants when they are dormant or inactive. Herbaceous plants that bloom in spring and die by midsummer can be moved after the leaves have yellowed; late summer and fall bloomers are best moved in early spring.

When planting near existing trees, dig large planting holes and remove all roots so that the new shrubs and wildflowers have a chance to get established. Plant in prepared soil, and use time-released fertilizer tablets with larger plants if desired. Mulch all new plantings with leaf litter or wood chips to protect them from extremes of heat, cold, and drought, and watch them carefully through the first season.

Maintenance

Your principal maintenance tasks during the first two or three years will be to remove weeds and add mulch. During this time you'll probably also be adding new plants and continuing to expand and improve the garden.

Additional maintenance tasks may include some pruning to train young trees and shrubs; however, if you have spaced the plants with plenty of room to grow to their mature size, many will need no pruning at all. Do any heavy pruning or tree removal in winter. Watering can be important during prolonged dry periods, especially during the first several years when the plants are young. Continued mulching helps retain moisture and keep soil temperatures cool, in addition to enriching the soil. After several years, your forest garden should be producing most of its own mulch from fallen leaves.

Some forest floor perennials need division every several years. Do this in spring. Also in spring, you may give the garden a fertilization with a balanced fertilizer such as 10–10–10. Feed rhododendrons and other acid-loving plants with acid fertilizer.

Plants for forest gardens
Plants of Northeastern and Middle Atlantic Forests
(See the Central Forest list also; the Alleghenies and Cumberlands support the richest tree floras in the United States)

Trees

Acer rubrum	Red maple	Brilliant orange and scarlet fall color; streamsides to upland forest
Acer saccharum	Sugar maple	Golden fall color; excellent, long-lived shade tree
Betula papyrifera	Paper birch	White, papery bark; light yellow fall color
Carya ovata	Shagbark hickory	Gray bark peels in 1- to 3-inch slender strips; hickory nut of commerce
Liriodendron tulipifera	Tulip poplar	Large shade tree; tulip-shaped leaves and flowers
Pinus strobus	Eastern white pine	Large, 5-needle pine; excellent for windbreaks
Quercus alba	White oak	Large, slow-growing species; deep red fall color
Quercus coccinea	Scarlet oak	Small red oak with brilliant scarlet fall color
Quercus stellata	Post oak	Fall color dull yellow to brown; gravelly or sandy uplands
Tsuga canadensis	Hemlock	Cone-shaped, large evergreen; branches pendulous, cones less than 1 inch long

Shrubs

Amelanchier laevis	Allegheny shadblow	Small tree with showy white flowers in spring and purple to blackish berries in late summer
Aristolochia durior	Dutchman's pipe	Vine with curious, pipelike flowers
Chionanthus virginicus	Fringe-tree	Large shrub or small tree with greenish flowers and blue or black fruit; mostly on stream banks in nature
Cornus florida	Flowering dogwood	Small tree with very showy flowers
Fothergilla major	Large fothergilla	Profuse white flowers in spring
Hamamelis virginiana	Witch hazel	Yellow flowers in winter

Rhododendron species, including *atlanticum, calendulaceum, catawbiense, maximum, periclymenoides, prinophyllum, vaseyi,* and *viscosum:*

Viburnum prunifolium	Black haw	Shrub to small tree with white flowers and dark blue fruits; brilliant scarlet fall color
Viburnum trilobum	Highbush cranberry	Handsome shrubs with large red berries

Ferns

Adiantum pedatum	Maidenhair fern	Elegant fern with leaflets branching from 1- to 2-foot wiry stem
Osmunda cinnamomea	Cinnamon fern	Fronds turn cinnamon brown as spores ripen
Osmunda claytoniana	Interrupted fern	Edible fiddleheads

Forbs

Asarum canadense	Wild ginger	Reddish flowers that hide under heart-shaped leaves; excellent ground cover
Chrysogonum virginianum	Chrysogonum	Yellow daisy that blooms all summer
Cornus canadensis	Bunchberry	Ground cover with white dogwood flowers and red berries
Epigaea repens	Trailing arbutus	Showy ground cover; grows in moist peaty soils
Erythronium americanuum	Trout lily	Handsome yellow lily
Hepatica acutiloba and *H. americana*	Hepaticas	Leaves in 3 parts; masses of flowers in white to rose to lavender
Iris cristata	Dwarf crested iris	Handsome, purple flowered species
Jeffersonia diphylla	Twinleaf	Leaves resemble butterflies
Mertensia virginica	Virginia bluebells	Clusters of hanging flowers
Mitchella repens	Partridgeberry	White flowers, red berries
Phlox divaricata and *P. stolonifera*	Phlox	Light blue and red, respectively
Polygonatum biflorum	Solomon's seal	Tall, lilylike stems with blue berries
Sanguinaria canadensis	Bloodroot	One of earliest woodland plants to bloom
Shortia galacifolia	Oconee bells	Choice woodland plant; white, pink or blue
Smilacina stellata	Starry false Solomon's seal	Similar to Solomon's seal
Silene virginica	Fire pink	Five scarlet petals in star formation

Trillium species (*cernuum, erectum, grandiflorum,* and *undulatum*)

	Trilliums	Single stem with 3 leaves and 3 petals in white, pink, or purple

Left: Viburnum trilobum *(highbush cranberry)*. Above: Rhododendron calendulaceum.

Central Appalachian Forest
(See also Great Lakes Forest list)

Trees

Acer rubrum	Red maple	Tends to occur on wetter sites
Acer saccharum	Sugar maple	Especially with beech and basswood
Aesculus glabra	Ohio buckeye	Excellent shade tree
Betula lutea	Yellow birch	Especially on wetter sites
Carpinus caroliniana	Blue beech	Small tree with smooth, grayish bark
Carya species	Hickories	Present but not dominant in central Appalachians
Cladrastis lutea	Yellow-wood	Foot-long clusters of white, pea-shaped flowers
Fagus grandifolia	American beech	Stately tree with smooth, gray bark; dominant in much of the Central deciduous forest
Fraxinus americana	White ash	Excellent shade tree
Liriodendron tulipifera	Tulip tree	Large tree with tulip-shaped leaves and tuliplike green and yellow flowers

Quercus species (*alba, bicolor, macrocarpa,* and *rubra*)

	Oaks	See Great Lakes Forest list
Quercus shumardii	Shumard oak	Large red oak; excellent for shade
Quercus stellata	Post oak	Medium-sized upland white oak; also in deep South
Tilia americana	Basswood	Especially common in beech-maple forest

Shrubs
(same as Great Lakes and Northeastern Forest lists, except for the following replacements in genus *Crataegus*)

Crataegus marshallii	Parsley hawthorn	Also in deep South
Crataegus opaca	Mayhaw	Showy red fruits, also in deep South

Forbs

Actaea pachypoda and *A. rubra*	Baneberries	Autumn fruits very showy
Anemonella thalictroides	Rue anemone	Delicate white flowers
Aquilegia canadensis	Wild columbine	Yellow and orange flowers
Asarum canadense	Wild ginger	Excellent ground cover
Asarum shuttleworthi	Mottled wild ginger	Leaves mottled with white
Astilbe biternata	False goatsbeard	Feathery white flowers; to 6 feet tall
Hepatica americana	Round-lobed hepatica	Very early "May-baskets" of white, rose, or purple flowers
Iris verna	Vernal iris	Usually in acid soils; the smallest native iris
Isopyrum biternatum	False rue anemone	Forms large mats on the forest floor; delicate anemone flowers, dissected foliage
Jeffersonia diphylla	Twinleaf	Named for Thomas Jefferson; south only to Virginia
Mertensia virginica	Virginia bluebells	Also in sunny meadows
Phlox divaricata	Woodland phlox	Blue flowers; an essential species
Podophyllum peltatum	May apple	Looks like an umbrella; solitary white flower produces large green berry
Sanguinaria canadensis	Bloodroot	Very early white flowers with yellow centers
Shortia galacifolia	Oconee bells	Limited in natural range but very choice in the woodland garden
Tiarella cordifolia	Allegheny foamflower	Fluffy white wands from rosettes of scalloped round leaves; south only to North Carolina

Trillium species (*erectum, erectum album, grandiflorum, luteum, sessile, stylosum, undulatum,* and *viride*)

	Trilliums	A vernal visual feast in white, purple, pink, and yellow;

Uvularia species (*grandiflora, perfoliata,* and *sessilifolia*)

	Bellflowers	Pendant yellow flowers in spring
Viola pedata	Bird's foot violet	Sun or light shade

Left: Podyphyllum peltatum (*May apple*).

Center: Aquilegia canadense (*columbine*).

Above: Mertensia virginica (*Virginia bluebells*).

Southeastern Forests

Trees

Carya illinoinensis	Pecan	Edible nuts; to 150 feet
Carya tomentosa	Mockernut hickory	Handsome shade tree
Cercis canadensis	Redbud	Beautiful spring flowers
Cornus florida	Dogwood	A widely planted native
Franklinia altamaha	Franklinia	Tree in camellia family extinct in the wild since 1806; named for Benjamin Franklin
Ilex cassine	Cassine holly	Pale green foliage; large shrub to small tree
Ilex opaca	American holly	Bright red berries; pyramidal form
Juniperus virginiana	Eastern red cedar	Excellent for impoverished soils
Liquidambar styraciflua	American sweet gum	Showy autumn colors depending on cultivar; pendant, spiny spherical fruits
Magnolia acuminata	Cucumber magnolia	Flowers greenish; excellent shade tree
Magnolia grandiflora	Southern magnolia	White flowers to 8 inches across; shiny, dark, evergreen leaves
Magnolia macrophylla	Bigleaf magnolia	Leaves to 2½ feet long, 12 inches wide; flowers to 15 inches across; deciduous
Magnolia virginiana	Sweet bay magnolia	Flowers white and lemon-scented; semievergreen
Nyssa sylvatica	Black gum	Early scarlet fall color; "alligator" bark
Oxydendrum arboreum	Sourwood	Fragrant flowers resemble lily-of-the-valley
Persea borbonia	Red bay	Aromatic evergreen leaves used as cooking spice; relative of avocado
Pinus echinata	Shortleaf pine	Fairly fast-growing; plated bark on older specimens
Pinus elliotti	Slash pine	Grows on the poorest soil
Pinus palustris	Longleaf pine	Plumelike foliage; cones to 12 inches
Pinus taeda	Loblolly pine	Fast-growing, pioneer species; excellent shade for azaleas and dogwoods
Prunus caroliniana	Cherry laurel	Evergreen cherry; fruits attract birds
Quercus alba	White oak	Large, slow-growing species
Quercus falcata	Southern red oak	Popular shade tree in South; provides red fall color
Quercus nigra	Water oak	Tolerant of wide variety of soil conditions
Quercus phellos	Willow oak	Leaves like a willow
Quercus virginiana	Southern live oak	Quintessential tree of the South
Sabal palmetto	Cabbage palm	Hardy only in the deep South; state tree of Florida; edible young buds

Shrubs and Vines

Callicarpa americana	American beautyberry	Rose to purple berries persist after leaves drop
Calycanthus floridus	Carolina allspice	Aromatic foliage; reddish brown flowers
Clematis virginiana	Clematis	Flowers white; male and female flowers on separate plants
Fothergilla major	American witch-alder	Fluffy white late spring blooms with honeylike fragrance
Hydrangea quercifolia	Oakleaf hydrangea	Glorious red to purple autumn color
Ilex vomitoria	Yaupon	Translucent hollyberries; multiple stems produce "sculptured" form
Myrica cerifera	Southern wax myrtle	Fast and dense growth make for excellent hedging plant
Passiflora incarnata	Passion flower	Vine with exotic flowers; host plant of Gulf fritillary butterfly *Agraulis vanillae*
Rhododendron species *austrinum* and *canescens*	Flame azalea and wild honeysuckle, respectively	Need sun or partial shade; flowers yellow-orange and pink, respectively
Smilax lanceolata	Lanceleaf greenbriar	Vine; used for trellising and cut foliage in bouquets
Wisteria macrostachya	Wisteria	Vine; lavender flowers; large pendant fruits

Forbs

See Central Forest list. Wildflowers of the Southern forests are very similar.

Great Lakes Forest

Trees

Acer saccharum	Sugar maple	Golden in fall; widely planted for shade and bright orange-red fall color
Amelanchier canadensis	Serviceberry	Earliest *Amelanchier* to blossom
Amelanchier laevis	Allegheny shadblow	Showy white flowers in spring
Betula lutea	Yellow birch	Peeling, yellowish bark; often on river flood plains but adaptable to drier sites
Carpinus caroliniana	Blue beech	Small with smooth, grayish bark; bright scarlet and orange fall color

Left: Liriodendron tulipifera (*tulip tree*).   Above: Acer saccharum (*sugar maple*).

Carya ovata	Shagbark hickory	Large, with edible nuts; grows in uplands with oaks
Fagus grandifolia	Beech	Large, with smooth gray bark; often with sugar maple and tulip tree
Fraxinus americana	White ash	Large; yellow or purple fall color; on rich soils of bottomlands
Gleditsia triacanthos (also cultivars)	Honey locust	Long, twisted seed pods; pale yellow fall color
Gymnocladus dioica	Kentucky coffee tree	Short, heavy seed pods, ground for coffee substitute in 18th and 19th centuries
Larix laricina	Tamarack	Pyramidal, deciduous conifer; wide range of habitats from uplands to swamps
Liriodendron tulipifera	Tulip tree	Tall and straight, with fissured bark and tuliplike leaves and flowers
Ostrya virginiana	Ironwood	Understory tree; elmlike leaves; yellow fall color
Pinus resinosa	Red pine	Medium-sized, 2-needle pine with reddish bark and 2-inch cones
Pinus strobus	Eastern white pine	Large, 5-needle pine, to 8 inches; widely planted
Plantanus occidentalis	Sycamore	Distinctive, plated bark; often branches into several trunks near the ground
Prunus serotina	Wild black cherry	Large with plated bark; yellow fall color
Quercus alba	Upland white oak	Very large and slow-growing; deep red fall color
Quercus bicolor	Swamp white oak	Large, fast-growing; yellow to orange fall color; excellent shade tree
Quercus macrocarpa	Bur oak	Large white oak; acorns surrounded by "fringe;" can be huge, especially in wet areas
Quercus rubra	Red oak	Large and fast-growing; brown to dull orange fall color; "streaked" pattern on branches
Tilia americana	Basswood	Large and excellent for shade; yellow fall color
Tsuga canadensis	Hemlock	Large, pyramidal evergreen; drooping branches; small cones
Alnus rugosa	Speckled alder	Small with showy catkins and cones; usually in swamps or on stream banks
Celastrus scandens	Bittersweet	Vine; bright orange berry clusters in fall; used in dried arrangements
Cornus alternifolia	Pagoda dogwood	Small flat-topped trees; branches in "pagodalike" tiers; yellow and scarlet fall color

Crataegus crus-galli (including thornless cultivars and species *punctata* and *mollis*)

	Hawthorne	Small; edible red berries; often grow at edge of forest and meadow
Diervilla lonicera	Dwarf honeysuckle	Yellow clusters of flowers; small shrub
Euonymus atropurpurea	Wahoo	Relative of bittersweet; bright red clusters of hanging capsules in fall
Hamamelis virginiana	Witch hazel	Forest-prairie edge as well as woods and stream banks; yellow flowers in fall
Juniperus communis	Common juniper	Small shrub with short needles that turn brown in winter; var. *depressa* is an excellent ground cover on poor soils
Malus coronaria and M. ioensis*	Crabapples	Small trees with showy pink to white flowers, and small yellow-green apples used in jellies
Physocarpus opulifolius	Ninebark	Spiraealike shrubs with exfoliating bark
Prunus americana	Wild plum	Small; showy white to pink flowers; bright red fruits used in jams and jellies
Rhus typhina	Staghorn sumac	Small; fruit clusters cinnamon brown; intense scarlet fall color

Shrubs

Viburnum lentago	Nannyberry	Dark blue berries; usually on forest edge; orange to red fall color
Viburnum trilobum	Highbush cranberry	Large red berries
Actaea pachypoda and A. rubra*	Baneberries	2- to 3-foot plants with showy berries in fall

Forbs

Anemonella thalictroides	Rue anemone	Delicate white anemones in early spring; grows from small tuber
Aquilegia canadensis	Columbine	Attractive hanging yellow and red flowers in summer
Arisaema atrorubens	Jack-in-the-pulpit	Showy, unusual flowers; edible roots; bright scarlet fruit clusters in fall
Asarum canadense	Wild ginger	Excellent ground cover with heart-shaped leaves
Aster macrophyllus	Big-leaved aster	Subtle; leaves very large and basal
Erythronium albidum and E. americanum*	Trout lilies	White and yellow lilies, on 4- to 8-inch stems
Geranium maculatum	Wild geranium	Generous blooms in light pink or purple; will tolerate some sun
Hepatica acutiloba and H. americana*	Hepaticas	"Maybaskets" of attractive 3-parted leathery leaves and masses of flowers in white, pink, blue, or purple
Isopyrum biternatum	False rue anemone	Similar to *Anemonella*
Jeffersonia diphylla	Twinleaf	Leaves butterfly-shaped; forms clumps about 2 feet tall
Mertensia virginica	Virginia bluebells	Blue, hanging bell-shaped flowers; sun or light shade

Pacific Forests

Trees

Abies concolor	White fir	Large (to 250 feet in Sierras); frequently planted; bears upright cones
Acer macrophyllum	Big-leaf maple	Large, deeply divided leaves; bright orange fall color; on stream banks and bottomlands
Alnus species (including species *rubra, rhombifolia,* and *sinuata*)		
	Alders	30–40 foot trees with grayish bark; on stream banks and in mountain canyons
Calocedrus decurrens	Incense cedar	Tall, tapering evergreen 100–150 feet; widely planted
Chamaecyparis lawsoniana (also cultivars)	Port Orford cedar	To 200 feet; widely planted, with most natural groves near Oregon and California coasts
Lithocarpus densiflorus	Tanbark oak	80–150 feet; abundant in coastal redwood belt; intermediate between oaks and chestnuts
Pinus lambertiana	Sugar pine	200-foot pyramidal tree bearing large cones to 18 inches long; sweet substance exudes from broken heartwood
Pinus monticola	Western white pine	10–150 feet, cones to 11 inches; scattered throughout the Northwest
Pinus ponderosa	Ponderosa pine	To 230 feet; cinnamon-red bark; widely planted; usually on dry sites
Pseudotsuga menziesii	Douglas fir	To 200 feet; blue-green foliage; seeds have "prongs" that stick out from the cones
Quercus agrifolia	Coast live oak	To 90 feet; leaves oval and toothed; acorns to 1½ inches long; evergreen
Quercus chrysolepis	Canyon live oak	To 50 feet, bearing great horizontal branches forming a canopy to 150 feet across; evergreen
Quercus kelloggii	California black oak	To 100 feet; deciduous with yellow or brown fall color; acorns to 1½ inches
Sequoia sempervirens	Redwood	To 340 feet; within 20–30 miles of the coast in nature but widely planted; cones very small
Tsuga mertensiana	Mountain hemlock	To 150 feet; branches drooping; oval, cylindric cones to 3 inches
Umbellularia californica	California bay	75–150 feet; leaves yellow to orange in fall but since most live several seasons, tree appears green year-round; leaves very aromatic

Shrubs

Acer circinatum	Vine maple	Leaves similar to Japanese maple; 30–40 feet; rich orange to scarlet fall color
Amelanchier alnifolia	Saskatoon berry	To 40 feet; white flowers in spring; fruit dark blue and edible
Andromeda polifolia	Bog rosemary	Needs mulch of sphagnum peat
Cornus nuttallii (including cultivars)	Pacific flowering dogwood	Small tree 40–60 feet; "petals" to 3 inches long, white or tinged with pink; clusters of 30–40 scarlet berries
Corylus cornuta, including var. *californica*	Hazel	Shrub to 15 feet; needs moisture
Garrya fremontii	Silk tassel bush	Hanging clusters of male and female flowers; shrub to 10 feet
Gaultheria shallon	Salal	Small shrub with shiny, light green leaves and white to rose waxy, urnlike flowers in clusters
Holodiscus discolor	Oceanspray	Shrub to 15 feet; dense clusters of small white to pink flowers
Physocarpus capitatus	Ninebark	Small shrub with peeling bark, white flowers
Quercus garryana	Oregon post oak	Deciduous tree to 60 feet; see chaparral-oak woodland list for other oaks
Rhamnus purshiana	Cascara	To 40 feet; deciduous; yellow fall color; in rich coniferous forest
Rhododendron macrophyllum	California rose-bay	Clusters of rose to rose-purple flowers; leaves to 9 inches long; evergreen
Rhododendron occidentale	Western azalea	Shrub to 15 feet; clusters of showy white flowers, often with pink blush
Ribes sanguineum	Red flowering currant	To 12 feet; leaves green and whitish below; flowers pale to deep rose; dark berries
Vaccinium ovatum	Evergreen huckleberry	To 6 feet; leaves shiny and leathery; flowers white to pink; berries black

Ferns

Adiantum pedatum	Maidenhair fern	Delicate leaves on 1- to 2-foot leafless stalk
Asplenium trichomanes	Spleenwort	Small woodland fern
Athyrium filix-femina	Lady fern	Large, showy fern with both coastal and mountain varieties
Polystichum munitum	Sword fern	Showy, dark green fern; abundant under redwoods
Woodwardia fimbriata	Chain fern	Large handsome species; needs moist conditions

Forbs

Aconitum columbianum	Monkshood	Dark blue flowers on 3- to 5-foot stalks; similar to delphinium
Aquilegia formosa	Columbine	Edge and moist woods; red and yellow hanging flowers
Asarum caudatum and *A. hartwegii*	Wild ginger	Excellent ground covers; heart-shaped leaves, mottled in *A. hartwegii*
Clintonia uniflora	Queen's cup	Large, oval basal leaves; small white flowers and blue berries
Dicentra formosa (including var. *oregana*)	Bleeding heart	Rose flowers and fern-like foliage
Disporum smithii	Fairy bell	Coastal; branched stem bears whitish flowers and reddish berries
Erythronium oregonum and *E. revolutum*	Fawn lilies	Flowers pink outside and yellow or rose within, respectively
Linnaea borealis	Twinflower	Excellent ground cover
Smilacina racemosa	False Solomon's seal	Terminal clusters of bright red berries in fall
Trillium species (including species *chloropetalum, ovatum,* and *rivale*)		
	Trilliums	Flowers white fading to pink; first two to 24 inches; *T. rivale* is tiny
Vancouveria hexandra and *V. chrysantha* and *V. planipetala*		
	Inside-out flower	Fernlike plants with white flowers (yellow in *V. chrysantha*)

Above: Gaultheria shallon (*Wintergreen*).

Left: Umbellularia californica (*California bay laurel*).

Rocky Mountain Forests

Trees

Abies concolor	White fir	High elevations; 5-inch green-purple cones
Abies lasiocarpa	Subalpine fir	High elevations; to 100 feet or more
Acer glabrum	Rocky Mountain maple	Small; scarlet in fall
Amelanchier alnifolia and *Amelanchier utahensis*	Shadblow	Attractive white flowers, dark blue berries
Juniperus scopulorum	Rocky Mountain juniper	Dry sites; to 30 feet or more
Picea engelmannii	Engelmann spruce	Rich, loamy soils; blue-green leaves
Picea pungens	Blue spruce	Streamsides in nature; blue-green leaves
Pinus aristata	Bristlecone pine	Good for poor soils; 10–40 feet
Pinus flexilis	Limber pine	To 50 feet, branches drooping
Pinus ponderosa var. *scopulorum*	Ponderosa pine	Cinnamon-red, platelike bark, large and stately
Populus sargentii	Plains cottonwood	Widely grown shade tree
Populus tremuloides	Quaking aspen	Golden in fall; smooth, gray bark
Pseudotsuga menziesii	Douglas fir	Drought resistant; to 300 feet, but usually smaller

Shrubs

Artemisia tridentata	Big sagebrush	Silvery-gray and strongly aromatic
Cornus sericea	Red-osier dogwood	Bright red branches
Cowania mexicana	Cliff rose	Flowers white or yellow; to 7 feet
Crataegus douglasii	Western hawthorn	Fruit black and sweet
Prunus americana	American plum	Good jelly fruit; coarse tree or shrub
Prunus pensylvanica	Wild red cherry	Good for jellies; to 35 feet
Quercus gambelii	Gambel's oak	Golden fall color
Sambucus glauca	Blueberry elder	Fruits blue and sweet, used in jellies and pies
Shepherdia argentea	Silver buffalo berry	Leaves oblong and silver on both sides

Forbs (for planting in sunny areas; relatively few Rocky Mountain wildflowers are available for planting under trees)

Anemone patens	Pasqueflower	Showy purple flowers
Aquilegia caerulea	Rocky Mountain columbine	State flower of Colorado, large purple and white flowers
Camassia quamash	Common camas	Bulbs were important in the diets of Rocky Mountain region natives
Castilleja miniata; also *C. suphurea*	Indian Paintbrush	Orange and yellow, respectively; sow seeds with prairie grasses or in bluegrass sod; roots are semiparisitic on other plants' roots plants, especially grasses
Eriogonum umbellatum	Sulphur flower	Bright yellow flowers; forms loose mats to 1 foot height
Hymenoxys grandiflora	The old-man-of-the-mountains	4-inch sunflowers on a 6-inch plant
Iris missouriensis	Wild iris	Long light lilac or white-veined lilac-purple flowers
Leucocrinum montanum	Sand lily	Will grow in a variety of soils
Lewisia rediviva	Bitter-root	State flower of Montana, showy flowers; roots were food staple to native Americans
Liatris ligulistylis and *L. punctata*	Blazing-star	Purple blooms in late summer and autumn
Penstemon barbatus	Scarlet bugler	Hummingbird flower
Penstemon secundiflorus	Penstemon	Dark blue to red violet
Sedum species	Stonecrop	Succulents; see local manuals for species native to your area
Thermopsis pinetorum	Golden banner	All thermopsis are similar and valuable for both foliage and flowers

For more information about plants for forest gardens

Northeastern & Middle-Atlantic Forest Gardens

Growing Woodland Plants, by Clarence and Eleanor G. Birdseye. Dover Publications, Inc., New York, NY. 1972.

The New Wild Flowers and How to Grow Them, by Edwin F. Steffek. Timber Press, Portland, OR. 1983. (Sponsored by the New England Wild Flower Society, Framingham, MA.)

Central Appalachian Forest Gardens

Deciduous Forests of Eastern North Americas, by E. Lucy Braun. Blakiston Co., Inc., Philadelphia, PA. 1950.

Contains detailed descriptions of individual forests, particularly with regard to the geographic distribution of tree species, throughout the eastern United States.

Great Lakes Forest Gardens

The Vegetation of Wisconsin, An Ordination of Plant Communities, by T. John Curtis. University of Wisconsin Press, Madison, WI. 1959.

Extensive descriptions of plant communities of Wisconsin, as well as plant lists. Basically this is an ecological text, and not a flora.

Plants of the Chicago Region: A Checklist of the Vascular Flora of the Chicago Region, with Keys; Notes on Local Distribution, Ecology, and Taxonomy; and a System for Evaluation of Plant Communities, Third Edition, by Floyd Swink and Gerould Wilhelm. The Morton Arboretum, Lisle, IL. 1979.

Lists, keys, and maps all known plants with some of their associates for a 22-county area of Wisconsin, Illinois, Indiana, and Michigan centered around the city of Chicago. Perhaps the most comprehensive checklist available for any flora in the United States.

Southeastern Forest Gardens

Louisiana Trees and Shrubs, by Clair A. Brown. Claitor's Publishing Division, Baton Rouge, LA. 1965.

Illustrated guide to trees and shrubs of Louisiana. Most of these species range widely throughout the South.

Manual of the Vascular Flora of the Carolinas, by Albert E. Radford, Harry E. Ahles, and C. Ritchie Bell. University of North Carolina Press, Chapel Hill, NC. 1968.

Alpine of the Americas, The Report of the First Interim International Rock Garden Plant Conference in Seattle and Vancouver, July 18-25, 1976. Sharon Sutton, Editor. The American Rock Garden Society, Seattle, WA. 1978.

The published proceedings of the American Rock Garden Society's bicentennial tribute to the wildflowers of the Americas, including excellent color photographs. Many of the presentations are by authors of major reference works on North American wildflowers.

Pacific Forest Gardens

Gardening with Native Plants of the Pacific Northwest, An Illustrated Guide, by Arthur R. Kruckeberg. University of Washington Press, Seattle, WA and London, England. 1982.

A generously illustrated guide to landscaping with plants of the Pacific Northwest. Strongly conservation oriented, Kruckeberg notes rare species of special concern which should never be collected in the wild, such as Lewisia tweedyi, as well as providing information on how to grow common, horticulturally valuable species.

Flora of the Pacific Northwest, by C. L. Hitchcock and Arthur Cronquist. University of Washington Press, Seattle, WA. 1973.

Meadow gardens

Meadows are grasslands found in forested regions—the open patches of grasses and wildflowers common to the Eastern forests, the montane forests of the Rocky Mountains and the Sierra-Cascade ranges, and the Pacific coastal forest.

A meadow is a full-sun environment. Nearly all meadow plants require a bright, sunny exposure, and will not do well in shade. Each species also has fairly specific moisture preferences, growing best on either dry, moist, or saturated soils. Thus some meadow plants are usually found in wet meadows near streams or bogs, and others in dry, upland meadows.

Meadows are in constant transition. Changes occur in the predominant flower colors, plant heights, and landscape character throughout the season. Birds, butterflies, and other insects abound in a meadow. Insects that pollinate meadow flowers include many brightly colored and unusual moths and butterflies. Hummingbirds will be attracted by red, tubular flowers, such as penstemons. The ripening seed of meadow grasses will bring other birds, and some will stay to build nests on the ground amid the tall meadow plants.

If you are thinking of planting a meadow, see someone else's planting, if possible, to decide what you want and don't want in your own. And don't take on too big a project the first year; start with a small part of your garden, and gradually expand the meadow over several seasons.

Design

In planning your meadow, set aside a large, open area, such as a field or sunny slope, or you can plant islands of meadow grasses and wildflowers among the established plants and areas of your garden. Even if you will be planting a large area, you can spread the job over several years.

Your plant choices are many. The best species to choose will be those native to your region but, within those limits, you can choose from many attractive wildflowers and grasses. You may want to combine both wildflowers and grasses to imi-

Russell lupine and oxeye daisies have escaped from cultivation and naturalized to create a "neo-native" meadow that looks like a native one.

tate a natural meadow or just to create a brilliant tapestry of wildflowers.

Design the edge of the meadow carefully. If it is bordered by a forest or woodland, an irregular row of shrubs at the edge of the grasses will blend well with the forest trees, and will also help keep their seedlings from taking root in the meadow. An edge planting of densely rooted perennials such as aster, goldenrod, or hay-scented fern, will also discourage seedlings from invading at the periphery of the meadow.

Position the plant species on your plan according to their moisture preferences. If you have a wet spot, use it for water-loving iris or skunk cabbage; save the dry spots for species that can drown in too much moisture.

Choose wildflowers that will give you a succession of bloom from early spring to late fall. Either seed them at random for the most natural appearance, or plant certain wildflowers where you want to provide seasonal focal points and displays of color. When choosing flowering plants, remember that annual flowers will bloom the first year from seed, but perennials will usually not bloom until the second or third season. Well-adapted perennials are often a much better investment than annuals, because they will persist·in the garden; annuals, on the other hand, may reseed themselves for a few seasons, but will sometimes die out after that.

Soil preparation

When preparing a meadow soil, add as much organic soil amendment (such as peat, manure, or compost) as possible, to increase soil fertility and water retention. Use either the small-scale method of improving pockets of soil within the garden area, or dig in soil amendments over the entire area at one time.

Using the pocket improvement method, you can amend the soil and plant your meadow over several seasons, depending on its size. Dig up small spots within the garden area, spade in soil amendments, and sow seeds or set out plants there. The next year you can improve more areas, until eventually you have established the meadow. If you are creating a meadow on the site of an existing lawn, you can let lawn grasses grow unmowed to become meadow grasses. Plant small stands of

wildflower plants thoughout the grasses in areas of improved soil. If you want to use native grasses, kill the lawn grass with an herbicide before planting.

If you want to plant a meadow all in one season, improve the entire soil area at one time. Begin by killing any difficult, persistent weeds with a systemic herbicide. Then add ample organic matter to the soil and till it in. If there are many weed seeds in the soil, germinate them by keeping the soil moist, and kill them with an herbicide or shallow cultivation as they appear. Don't till deeply or you will bring more weed seeds to the surface.

Planting

Whether you start your meadow from seed or plants depends on the size of the meadow, your patience, and your budget. Many grasses and wildflowers are easiest to obtain as seed, and will germinate and grow readily on most sites.

If you plan a meadow of both grasses and forbs, you can sow the blended seed of all the grasses and forbs together at one time, or you can sow the grasses first and add the forbs later as seed or seedlings. This second method allows you to propagate the forbs ahead of time in flats or pots, and place them where you want them in the garden later.

Starting a meadow from seed

To obtain your blend of wildflowers, or wildflowers and grasses, you can buy the seed of individual meadow plants and make your own seed mixture. It is often easier, however, to buy one of the seed mixes that are widely sold by seed companies. If you do, see the notes on wildflower seed mixes on page 42. Because many seed mixes contain only wildflowers, you may wish to add a selection of the native grasses of your region to the mix.

How much seed should you sow? The best recommendation to follow is usually that of the supplier, but here are some average rates: for a mixed meadow of grasses and forbs, sow about 1 pound of grass seed and 1 ounce of wildflower seed per 1,000 square feet, or 10 to 15 pounds of grass seed and 10 to 40 ounces of wildflower seed per acre. For a pure stand of wildflowers sow 8 to 12 pounds per acre of most species. The higher rates of seeding will give a more lush meadow, but it may need supplemental water.

In mild-winter climates, sow the seed in summer or fall. In cold-winter climates, sow in fall if you need to overcome seed dormancy, or in spring if the seed has been treated to break dormancy. Mix the seed with sand or sawdust and hand-broadcast it evenly on a windless day. Rake it in lightly, and roll it if your site is small. Then cover it with ¼ inch of fine soil, organic material, or weed-free hay or straw.

For slopes or areas prone to high winds, a "binder" is available from some suppliers to apply with the seed. This substance, once it is lightly watered, holds the seed to the soil.

Setting out plants

Wildflower plants can be grown ahead and set out into the meadow as seedlings. Most grass species do not need this treatment and can be quite difficult to transplant, so plan to sow them directly on the site. Some wildflowers, however, are slow to germinate, or the seed is valuable. These will be worth the care of raising separately. Start to propagate the forbs in flats or pots early in the process, at about the time you sow the grass seed. Use seed, cuttings, or even divisions if available. Begin them in the fall or spring, then plant them in autumn, when they are a few inches tall. If you are following a planned layout for your meadow, rather than just planting it at random, lay out the paths before setting out the wild-flower plants. Then open up areas in the grasses, and plant the forb seedlings. Mulch all plantings with several inches of organic material.

Maintenance

A meadow is dramatic, changing with the seasons. Yours will take several years to establish its own blend of species. During this time, some species will die out and others will thrive and multiply.

Your major maintenance task in this early period is weeding, mostly by hand pulling. The weeds, especially the seedlings of woody plants, will be easiest to remove if you get them early. A weed is any plant you don't want in your meadow.

You may want to do some pruning of spent flowering stalks and dormant plants. You'll probably do less

of this as you live with your meadow and discover the beauty of dry flower stems and seed capsules in the winter. Leave the seed stalks of those species that keep their seeds into winter, to provide forage for birds.

A meadow needs to be cut early each spring to a height of about four inches. This kills most woody plant seedlings that have invaded it and it is essential in meadows bordered by forests, where the number of such

seedlings will be greater. You will probably need to rent a sicklebar mower or a scythe; conventional mowers will not cut woody vegetation. If there are paths through your meadow, mow them regularly to keep them open.

You may also wish to fertilize once a year to bring about more vigorous plant growth. Fertilize in the spring using a balanced fertilizer such as 10–10–10 or dried manure.

A steep hillside near Boston has become a charming meadow. Many of the native and non-native plants that grow here were seeded by being "pitched over the side" of the wall above.

A beautiful patch of naturalized exotics and natives in the corner of a prairie garden. Queen Anne's lace, feverfew (small white daisies), and coneflower seem to fit right in with the "true native" Ratibida, Liatris, and goldenrod (in bud at the bottom of the photo).

Plants for meadow gardens
Eastern Meadows
For more information about plants for meadow gardens, see the the books listed under Forest Gardens, in the previous section.

Grasses

Andropogon scoparius	Little bluestem	2–3 feet; bright red fall color
Andropogon virginicus	Broom sedge	Similar to little bluestem; not as colorful in fall
Bouteloua curtipendula	Side-oats grama	2–3 feet; some clones are sod-formers, others cluster in bunches
Koeleria cristata	Junegrass	Showy inflorescences; glossy spikelike panicles

Forbs

Asclepias tuberosa	Butterflyweed	Bright orange flowers
Aster novae-angliae	New England aster	Showy purple flowers with yellow centers
Baptisia australis	Blue baptisia	Large blue legume flowers
Baptisia tinctoria	Yellow baptisia	Showy yellow flowers; 2–3 feet
Bidens aristosa	Tickseed-sunflower	Showy yellow "sunflowers" with yellow centers; prefers wet meadows
Coreopsis lanceolata	Lance-leaved coreopsis	1–2 feet; bright yellow flowers; dry or sandy soils
Dodecatheon meadia	Shooting-star	Clusters of showy flowers with bright pink reflexed petals
Echinacea purpurea	Purple coneflower	Purple sunflowers
Eryngium yuccifolium	Rattlesnake master	Leaves like a yucca; umbels of spherical flower clusters
Eupatorium maculatum and *E. purpureum*	Joe-pye weed	Purple flowers
Filipendula rubra	Queen-of-the-prairie	Very showy clusters of delicate pink flowers
Helianthus tuberosus	Jerusalem artichoke	Sunflower; very invasive; a species to be very careful with
Iris versicolor	Wild blue flag	Blue flowers; 3 feet tall
Krigia biflora	Two-flowered Cynthia	Flowers deep orange; leaves glaucous, mostly basal, and blue-green
Liatris pycnostachya	Prairie gayfeather	Purple spikes of this and the similar *L. spicata* can be bought as cut flowers
Lilium canadense	Wild yellow lily	Orange-yellow to red spotted flowers
Lilium michiganense	Michigan lily	Whorled leaves, orange-red spotted flowers
Lilium martagon	Turk's cap lily	Purple flowers, spotted with black
Lilium philadelphicum	Prairie or wood lily	Showy yellow and red-orange; one of the finest plants in North America
Lupinus perennis	Lupine	Showy bluish flowers
Mertensia virginica	Virginia bluebells	In meadows and woods, blooms when morel mushrooms are up
Monarda didyma	Scarlet beebalm	Showy scarlet "pompoms"
Monarda fistulosa	Wild bergamot	Lavender flowers; plants aromatic
Rhexia mariana and *R. virginica*	Meadow beauty	Flowers pale pink and deep, vivid pink respectively; very beautiful
Rudbeckia triloba	Thin-leaved coneflower	Showy clusters of small, golden sunflowers
Solidago nemoralis	Oldfield goldenrod	Soft golden flowers
Solidago speciosa	Showy goldenrod	In late fall produces golden plumes
Veronicastrum virginicum	Culver's root	Flowers are slender clusters of vertical white spires
Viola pedata	Bird's foot violet	Choice dwarf "pansy," but only for dry, sterile soils
Zizia aurea	Golden Alexanders	Showy yellow umbels

Grasses should take up 50 to 80 percent of the ground area in a prairie garden, as they do in a real prairie, though wildflowers are more obvious. Without the grasses as support, prairie forbs would appear leggy and might topple.

Prairie gardens

Historically, prairie extended south from the plains of central Canada to Texas, and from Illinois westward to Colorado and Montana. This region was once covered by the dominant grasses and bright forbs of prairie vegetation. Remnants of prairie are all that now remain, scattered in state parks, wildlife refuges, and along railroad rights-of-way.

The prairie landscape is one of hardy, deep-rooted plants, well-adapted to the wind, drought, heat, and cold. If you live in the prairie or plains region, your landscaping can preserve the beauty of these plants and bring a rich tapestry of ever-changing form and color to your garden. A prairie garden is remarkably stable. The plants reach deep into the soil for water and nutrients, so require little watering or fertilization once established. A prairie needs occasional weeding in its early years; after this, it can do with an infrequent mowing or burning. The energy and time needed to maintain a prairie garden is far less than that needed for a conventional landscape.

Design

You cannot create a replica of the prairie in a small yard. The sweep and diversity of the prairie requires several acres to unfold. But even on a smaller lot, you can represent the prairie in miniature by planting prairie grasses and forbs.

Begin your garden design with a site analysis. Note especially the available soil moisture in each area, and whether any areas are shaded.

These shady areas will need woodland or forest vegetation—prairie plants require full sun.

Use any existing site features in your design: buildings, fences, rocks, and especially such topographic features as slopes and *swales* (low spots in rolling terrain). Emphasize this topography, if you wish, by digging out the swales and adding the excavated soil to the tops of the slopes.

Decide where paths should go; these can be mowed grass or gravel. Wood chips, though often used for paths, can bring in weed seeds.

Bear in mind that a prairie is a grassland, with 50 to 80 percent of the ground area covered by grasses. When ordering seed, stay within this range, planning a ratio of about 70 percent grass to 30 percent forbs. Expect the grasses to gradually cover more ground than this. Though it may be tempting to order and plant just wildflowers, leaving out the less colorful grasses, the grasses serve a number of important functions, including providing physical support for some of the taller prairie forbs, which otherwise can become overgrown and leggy.

For the best visual effect, choose just a few species for a small prairie garden—perhaps 2 or 3 grasses combined with 10 or 12 forbs for an area that is only a few thousand square feet in size. For a large prairie planting, combine grass and forb species in greater numbers to mirror the true prairie diversity.

Match plants to the habitats of your site, especially to the available moisture in each garden area. Some prairie plants grow best on dry sites; others prefer moist or wet soils. Most prairie forbs and grasses are not particular about soil texture, but a few do best on sandy, well-drained soils, and will not do well in clay.

If your property is small, consider sharing a prairie garden with a neighbor; or, if you live in a development with common areas, inquire about planting some of these areas with prairie vegetation. Other ways to plant prairie species in a small yard are to plant islands of prairie species within a traditionally kept lawn area or to use prairie grasses as the background for a perennial flower bed. In both cases, use the smaller prairie plants, such as little bluestem or prairie dropseed, and the forbs with finer leaf textures such as purple prairie clover and shooting-star.

Design the prairie planting in sweeps and drifts of single species. Plant one or two species to be dominant in one area, gradually blending them with other dominant plants in adjacent areas. Plant only small numbers of any species that is an aggressive clump-former or runner, lest it take over the garden.

Keep plant heights in mind when planning the garden. Place the tallest plants at the center of the garden, away from paths and building windows. Use lower-growing species along paths and at the edges of the prairie. One exception to this is that some warm-season prairie grasses (such as little bluestem and Indian grass) can be attractive foundation plantings along the house.

Site and soil preparation

To prepare the site, first make any topographic changes you've planned. Then remove persistent weeds with a non-persistent systemic herbicide. Improvement of soil fertility may be necessary on sites where the topsoil has been removed or compacted with heavy equipment (such as around a new home). In these situations, you can work manure, compost, or leaf mold into the soil. In most cases, however, soil improvement is unnecessary. The best strategy for most gardens is to analyze your soils and plant habitats, and choose prairie plants tolerant of these conditions. Many prairie plants will respond to high soil fertility by becoming overly large and coarse.

If only part of your property is in full sun, choose that area for your corner of prairie. Here a gardener has both worlds, with a prairie in the foreground and a forest behind.

After the soil is graded and tilled, keep it moist for several weeks to germinate any weed seeds that may be present. Kill the seedlings with an herbicide or shallow cultivation.

Sowing and planting

Don't collect your prairie plants in the wild. Because of their extensive root systems, it is very unlikely you'll dig up enough root for a successful transplanting. The plant may live in your garden for a season, drawing on its past reserves, but then it usually will die. Even if it continues living, it may never do well enough to reproduce.

Instead of collecting in the wild, order seed or plants from a supplier of prairie plants or collect seed or cuttings in the wild. These methods will give you a better chance of success.

It is especially important to order prairie seed and plants from local sources or the nearest source you can find. In nature, the prairie extends across widely varying environments, from Canada to Texas, so there is tremendous variation even within individual species. Prairie dropseed plants grown in North Dakota, for example, will have different dates of flowering from prairie dropseed plants grown in Oklahoma, making each unsuited for garden use in the other region. Ordering plants or seed from a source far to the south of you may, in addition, bring plants of marginal hardiness into your garden; you could lose them the first winter. Plants or seed grown in other areas may also have difficulty adapting to your soils. For all these reasons, try to find local sources of seed and plants.

For most prairie or plains regions, the best sowing time is spring, when the weather has begun to warm (June in the North; earlier in the South). You can also sow in the fall, especially to prepare dormant seeds for germination with the alternate freezing and thawing of winter. Or you can stratify the seeds indoors over the winter and sow them in spring. This will give the best germination and avoid loss of seed to spring runoff.

Here is a method for sowing a prairie garden in a small area. Prepare and cultivate the area as discussed above. Mix the seed with some sand to permit more even sowing (the sand will also show where you've sown). Keep the seed of each species separate. Begin by broadcasting the dominant grasses over the entire area, then sow the forb seed where the design calls for each species. Try for a density of about 4 to 5 seeds per square foot. Rake the seeds in lightly and roll the area with a lawn roller. Consider using labeled stakes to mark the forb locations so they aren't pulled up by mistake later, during weeding. Keep the area moist by supplemental watering for a few weeks.

For large areas of an acre or more in size, hand-broadcasting of seed becomes impractical. Machinery designed specifically for grassland planting is available in some areas, including the Truax drill. Because this equipment seeds in regular rows, it is best to follow it with some spot-seeding of forbs, to give it a more natural appearance. Irrigation of large areas is not practical, so time the seeding to take place before the hot summer weather arrives.

Setting out plants is an economical alternative to sowing a prairie from seed only when the area is small or you have propagated the plants yourself. Otherwise it can be very expensive. If you are planting seedlings, set them out in the fall or early spring, when they are dormant.

Maintenance

The first three years are the critical maintenance period. The grasses will grow quickly, but the forbs more slowly. Don't be discouraged by the apparently slow growth of the prairie forbs. They slowly spread their roots into the soil, and only after two or more years of root growth do they make appreciable top growth. This process is essential to their hardiness, guaranteeing drought resistance and plant nutrition.

During the first three years, keep the prairie diligently weeded. Learn what the prairie plant seedlings look like to avoid pulling them with the weeds. If many weeds appear right after planting, mow the prairie at a height of 5 to 8 inches about 30 days after the seeding date.

About every three or four years, your prairie will benefit from mowing or burning, to control thatch and weeds and open up the soil surface. If the prairie is near buildings, or if burning is not permitted in your area, mow it to a height of 5 to 8 inches. Before mowing, rake off any thatch that has accumulated on the ground.

Where it is permitted, burning is preferable to mowing. Both burning and mowing remove thatch and thin excess growth, but burning also leaves a nutrient-rich layer of ash on the soil surface. Your first burn (or mowing) should be in the third or fourth year after planting. Don't plan to burn the entire prairie in one year; a method of burning half the area one year and half the next will make it easier to control the burn, and will better protect any small wildlife that has taken up residence in the prairie.

Plan your burn or mowing for early spring (April is best in many areas). This timing will kill most exotic weeds before they set seed for the year, and allow the sun to warm the soil, giving the warm-season grasses and forbs a head start on growth for the season. Choose a calm day for burning, or one with only a gentle breeze. Establish a firebreak by knocking down vegetation around the edge of the burn and wetting it thoroughly. Knock down all other upright growth in the prairie area with a rake. Have on hand several rakes, a water hose, and a "fire-slapper" of some type. This can be a snow shovel, or a custom-made tool consisting of a broad strip of rubber tire attached to a pole. Begin the burn at the downwind edge of the prairie, and let it burn upwind until it has burned the thatch and most of the vegetation. You will be surprised at how quickly and evenly your prairie garden will regrow after the burning.

In June, this stretch of virgin prairie is abloom with shooting stars and orange puccoon. Here, in July, Liatris pichifolia *dominates.*

Plants for prairie gardens
Northern Prairie

Shrubs
Amorpha canescens	Leadplant	Ash-colored foliage; flowers purple with yellow stamens
Ceanothus americanus	New Jersey tea	To 4 feet, bearing clusters of feathery, white flowers

Grasses
Andropogon gerardii	Big bluestem	Dominant species; to 6 feet in autumn; yellow, brown, and orange fall color
Andropogon scoparius	Little bluestem	Dry sites; to 3 feet; reddish fall color
Bouteloua curtipendula	Side-oats grama	Dry sites; to 3 feet; buffy fall color
Bouteloua gracilis	Blue grama	Stems in dense, erect clusters; to 20 inches
Elymus canadensis	Nodding Canada wild rye	Easy to establish; showy ryelike heads
Koeleria cristata	Junegrass	Warm season grass, to 18 inches; heads like timothy
Panicum virgatum	Switchgrass	Tall and aggressive; avoid overplanting
Sorghastrum nutans	Indiangrass	Dominant species; to 6 feet in autumn, with cinnamon heads
Sporobolus heterolepis	Northern dropseed	Considered the most beautiful prairie grass
Stipa spartea	Needlegrass	Warm season grass, to 3½ feet; sharp head of seed gives it its name

Forbs
Asclepias sullivantii	Sullivant's milkweed	Waxy bluish green leaves with pink midveins; pink flowers
Asclepias tuberosa	Butterflyweed	To 3 feet; showy orange flowers; long in cultivation
Asclepias verticillata	Horsetail milkweed	Showy flowers; easy to cultivate
Aster azureus	Sky blue aster	Light blue flowers, to 3 feet; arrow-shaped leaves
Aster laevis	Smooth aster	Smooth shiny leaves; light blue flowers with yellow centers; to 4 feet
Baptisia leucantha	White false indigo	To 4 feet, bearing tall white banners of white pea-flowers
Baptisia leucophaea	Cream false indigo	Low clumps to 2 feet tall; yellow pea flowers in low, lateral clusters; very showy
Cacalia tuberosa	Indian plantain	4–5 feet; sparse foliage; light green, shiny leaves
Camassia scilloides	Prairie hyacinth	Spring-blooming bulb producing light purple flowers
Coreopsis palmata	Prairie tickseed	To 2 feet, yellow "daisies" with yellow centers; forms large clumps
Echinacea pallida	Pale purple coneflower	6-inch purple "sunflowers" on 3-foot stalks
Echinacea purpurea	Purple coneflower	Prairie-forest edge; 6-inch dark purple sunflowers with orange centers
Eryngium yuccifolium	Rattlesnake-master	Yucca-like leaves
Filipendula rubra	Queen-of-the-prairie	Fragrant 6-foot herb with pink flowers resembling cotton candy; very beautiful
Gentiana andrewsii	Bottle gentian	Clusters of 2-inch purple "bottles" in 2-foot stems in fall
Gentiana puberula	Downy gentian	Open, upright, 5-pointed purple "chalices" in late fall; very choice
Ipomoea leptophylla	Bush morning-glory	Pink or purple 3-inch corolla; dry regions
Liatris aspera	Rough blazing-star	5-foot spikes of purple blooms in late summer or early fall
Liatris cylindracea	Cylindric blazing-star	3-foot spikes of lavender flowers; dry sites only
Liatris pycnostachya	Prairie blazing-star	5-foot plants bearing showy purple flower clusters, sold as cut flowers
Lithospermum canescens	Prairie puccoon	Clear orange fiddleheads on 1½ foot stems; very beautiful
Lobelia cardinalis	Cardinal flower	Wet, bright scarlet flowers on 5-foot stems; wet areas
Parthenium integrifolium	Wild quinine	To 4 feet; clusters of white flowers, used in dried arrangements
Penstemon digitalis	White-flowered penstemon	Floriferous; 4-foot tall white flowers
Petalostemon candidum	White prairie clover	To 3 feet; white flowers; dry sites
Petalostemon purpureum	Purple prairie clover	To 3 feet; purple flowers; mesic-to-dry sites

Phlox pilosa	Prairie phlox	2-foot clumps of bright pink flowers in spring
Physostegia virginiana	False dragonhead	Mint; 5-foot pink "snapdragons"
Polytaenia nuttallii	Prairie parsley	Dry sites only; white seeds are held on plants and provide late fall texture
Potentilla arguta	Prairie cinquefoil	Modest white flowers and showy rust seed heads; used in dried arrangements
Ratibida pinnata	Yellow coneflower	Very floriferous yellow daisy with drooping petals; one of best for bouquets
Rudbeckia subtomentosa	Sweet coneflower	Tall yellow daisy to 6 feet; floriferous and aromatic
Silphium laciniatum	Compass plant	A symbol of the prairie; to 14 feet; large yellow sunflowers on erect stems
Silphium terebinthinaceum	Prairie dock	Tall stems bearing clusters of small yellow daisies; basal "elephant-ear" leaves
Solidago rigida	Stiff goldenrod	Sulfur-yellow, flat-topped flower clusters turn to fluffy white in seed; easy to establish
Solidago speciosa	Showy goldenrod	4-foot golden plumes on wine-colored stems in late autumn; forms clumps
Veronicastrum virginicum	Culver's root	To 6 feet; clusters of white spikes at top of plant in late summer
Zizia aptera	Heart-leaved golden Alexanders	Short spring bloomer with waxy, showy leaves and yellow flower clusters
Zizia aurea	Golden Alexanders	To 3 feet; partial to moist sites; showy yellow flowers and shiny, dark green leaves

Palouse Prairie

Grasses

Andropogon smithii	Western wheatgrass	Erect stems to 2 feet or more
Bouteloua curtipendula	Side-oats grama	Stalks of pendant "oats"
Bouteloua gracilis	Blue grama	Dwarf species
Bromus marginatus	Western brome	Stems to 4 feet; closely flowered spikelets
Festuca idahoensis	Bluebunch fescue	
Koeleria cristata	Junegrass	Seed plumes similar to timothy
Oryzopsis hymenoides	Indian ricegrass	Large, feathery inflorescences
Sporobolus airoides	Alkali sacaton	Drought resistant
Stipa comata	Needle-and-thread	Stems to 2 feet or more; tufted; pale to brown

Forbs

Astragalus species	Milk vetch	Purple, white, or yellow flowers
Balsamorhiza sagittata	Arrowleaf balsamroot	Large "sunflowers," from rosettes of large basal leaves
Calochortus nuttallii	Sego lily	State flower of Utah
Camassia quamash	Camas	Moist meadows; flowers white to blue and blue-violet
Castilleja species	Paintbrush	
Clarkia pulchella	Beautiful Clarkia	Bright pink flowers
Gaillardia aristata	Blanketflower	Showy, "sunburst" sunflowers
Penstemon species	Penstemon	Inquire locally for species available
Sisyrinchium inflatum	Grass widow	Flowers lavender or purple, rarely white
Solidago species	Goldenrod	Inquire locally for species available
Sphaeralcea coccinea	Scarlet globe mallow	Orange-to-red showy flowers
Stanleya pinnata	Desert plume	Elegant wands of fluffy yellow flowers
Thermopsis montana	Golden banner	Handsome, golden flowers
Wyethia helianthoides	Mule's ears	White flowers

Above: Lithospermum canadense (*orange puccoon***) *blooms in spring.*

**Left: Ratibida *in a Wisconsin prairie in August.*

Above: Oenothera missouriensis (*Missouri primrose*).

Right: Andropogon gerardii (*big bluestem grass*).

High Plains

Shrubs and Small Trees
Artemisia tridentata	Big sagebrush	Silver-gray stems; to 10 feet; aromatic
Cercis occidentalis	Redbud	Fruits orange-red to dark purple; to 150 feet
Cercocarpus montanus	Mountain mahogany	Feathery seed plumes in fall
Eurotia lanata	Winter fat	Shrub with whitish "woolly" foliage
Juniperus scopulorum	Rocky Mountain juniper	Bluish; branches droop, soft foliage; dry, exposed sites
Rhus trilobata	Lemonade sumac	Berries used to make "lemonade"
Ribes odoratum	Golden currant	Yellow flowers have a clovelike fragrance
Sarcobatus vermiculatus	Greasewood	Gray bark, blue-green leaves

Grasses
Andropogon gerardii	Big bluestem	Plains strains are shorter than in the prairie proper
Andropogon scoparius	Little bluestem	Bright red fall color
Andropogon smithii	Western wheatgrass	
Buchloe dactyloides	Buffalograss	Very short species with separate male and female plants
Bouteloua gracilis	Blue grama	Excellent companion for the dwarf forbs
Bouteloua curtipendula	Side-oats grama	Ornamental hanging "oats"
Koeleria cristata	Junegrass	Warm season species which flowers early to mid-summer
Stipa comata	Needle-and-thread	Flowers in summer; to 2 feet or more

Forbs
Allium drummondii	Wild onion	
Amorpha canescens	Leadplant	Shrub with whitish foliage and purple flowers
Anemome patens	Pasqueflower	Early purple flowers, showy
Arnica fulgens	Arnica	Flowers golden, plant gray
Asclepias ovalifolia	Oval-leaved milkweed	Subtle; slender stems
Baptisia australis	Blue baptisia	Showy legume

Cacti (see pinyon-juniper and southern prairie lists—most of the species listed there range into the High Plains)

Callirhoe involucrata	Buffalo poppy	Large, crimson flowers
Castilleja species	Indian paintbrush	Sow seeds around prairie grasses such as *Andropogon scoparius*
Coreopsis tinctoria	Tickseed	Annual yellow "sunflower"
Delphinium virescens	Prairie larkspur	Flowers white, sometimes pale blue
Dodecatheon pulchellum	Shooting-star	Deep pink blooms; shady sites
Echinacea angustifolia	Purple coneflower	Very showy; flower rays are pink
Gaillardia aristata	Blanket flower	"Sunburst" flowers, widely grown in old-fashioned perennial gardens
Geum triflorum	Prairie smoke	Feathery seed heads
Ipomoea leptophylla	Bigroot bush morning glory	Gigantic tuberous roots; lavender flowers
Leucocrinum montanum	Sand lily	White lilies in spring; plant of alpine form
Liatris punctata	Blazing-star	Purple, shorter than Eastern species
Lilium philadelphicum	Prairie lily	Upright orange lilies
Oenothera missourensis	Missouri primrose	All the megapterium Oenotheras are spectacular, with large floppy flowers and great winged seedpods
Pediocactus simpsonii	Small cactus	Pink flowers, to 2 inches across
Penstemon angustifolius	Penstemon	Rich, light blue flowers; many other species available
Psoralea esculenta	Breadroot	Its starchy, tuberous roots were a staple in Plains Indians diets
Ratibida columnifera	Coneflower	Easy to establish; rays yellow or red
Townsendia exscapa and *T. hookeri*	Easter daisies	Stemless rosettes of white daisies
Yucca glauca	Great Plains yucca	Very variable, look for especially showy forms

Smooth sumac shows vivid fall color in an abandoned agricultural field. This area of Missouri is an ecotone, where prairie intermingles with areas of oak-hickory woods.

Central and Southern Prairie

Shrubs
(For prairie border and accents)

Bumelia lanuginosa	Buckthorn	Small shrub with fragrant flowers
Cercis canadensis	Redbud	Small tree bearing masses of light pink blooms in early spring
Dalea formosa and		
D. frutescens	Indigo bush	Small-leaved shrubs with bicolored purple and rose flowers
Hesperaloe parviflora	Real yucca	Blooms spring to midsummer on dry soils
Parkinsonia aculeata	Jerusalem thorn	Shrub or small tree to 40 feet, showy yellow flowers
Quercus macrocarpa	Bur oak	Can become large tree
Rhus aromatica	Sumac	Aromatic leaves; yellow flowers in spike clusters
Sophora secundiflora	Mescal bean	Scarlet beans are quite poisonous
Ungnadia speciosa	Spanish buckeye	Shrub or small tree with large flowers; seeds may be poisonous
Yucca glauca	Great Plains yucca	Stemless rosettes of basal leaves with 2- to 4-foot spikes of creamy white flowers in midsummer

Grasses
Eastern Texas and Oklahoma—same grasses as Northern Prairie
West Texas, Oklahoma Panhandle, and Eastern Colorado—same grasses as High Plains
Eastern New Mexico—grades into grasses of Southwest Grassland

Forbs

Allium stellatum	Wild onion	Pink flowers
Asclepias tuberosa	Butterflyweed	Showy orange or yellow flowers
Asclepias viridifolia	Green milkweed	Subtle; to nearly 3 feet
Aster kumleinii	Aster	Purple with gold centers
Astragalus species	Milk vetch	Many species, inquire locally for availability
Baptisia australis	Blue baptisia	Handsome flowers and form
Baptisia leucophaea	Cream baptisia	Very showy legume, inflated pods
Cucurbita foetidissima	Buffalo gourd	Vine; green and yellow striped fruit
Echinacea angustifolia	Purple coneflower	Purple "sunflower"
Echinocereus baileyi	Hedgehog cactus	See pinyon-juniper list for other species
Eustoma grandiflorum	Tulip gentian	Very showy purple flowers
Gilia rubra	Standing cypress	6-inch scarlet spikes
Liatris species *punctata,*		
pycnostachya, squarrosa	Blazing-star	Purple spikes in late summer and fall
Lupinus texensis	Bluebonnets	State flower of Texas
Mentzelia decapetala	Queen-of-the-plains	Large cream flowers; requires good drainage
Monarda fistulosa	Wild bergamot	Lavender; ranges over much of North America
Oenothera missourensis	Fluttermills	Large, lemon yellow flowers; papery winged pods
Oenothera speciosa	Evening primrose	Flowers white, rarely pink
Palafoxia hookerana	Othake rosywings	Limited natural distribution on sandy soils; showy pink flowers
Penstemon species *cobaea, grandiflorus,* and *secundiflorus*		
	Penstemon	Flowers white, rose, lavender, or purple depending on species
Petalostemon multiforus	Prairie clover	White
Petalostemon purpureum	Purple prairie clover	Purple; to 3 feet
Ratibida columnifera	Columan coneflower	Maroon or yellow rays
Salvia pitcheri	Blue sage	Abundant bloomer
Solidago mollis	Goldenrod	Gray leaves, gold flowers
Sphaeralcea coccinea	Scarlet mallow	Showy flowers

Southwestern (Semi-Desert) Grassland

(Grasslands of Trans-Pecos Texas, southern New Mexico, and southeastern Arizona) Fire suppression throughout all of the Southwest grasslands has resulted in the mass invasion of junipers, creosotebush, acacia, mesquites, and other shrubs into vast areas which were purely grassland at the time of the Spanish conquest. Overgrazing has also played a role in this degradation of the southwestern rangeland. In California, much coastal perennial grass prairie has been replaced by coastal sage chapparal, also as a result of fire suppression and overgrazing. Consequently, the communities we see today are very different from the original vegetation.

Small Trees, Shrubs, Cacti, and Stem Succulents

(Please refer to the Warm Desert list—plants of the southwestern desert grasslands and warm deserts often intermingle, with the grassland plants dropping out in the most arid sites)

Grasses

Bouteloua chondroisioides	Sprucetop grama	Important forage species
Bouteloua eriopoda	Black grama	Important forage species
Bouteloua filiformis	Slender grama	Slender sylphlike species, also important to grazing animals
Hilaria mutica	Tobosa grass	Blue-green; stems to 2 feet
Muhlenbergia porteri	Bush muhly	Feathery inflorescences

Forbs (including forbs of the warm deserts)

Abronia species	Sand verbena	Showy pink to white flowers, often in dry beds of desert streams
Baileya multiradiata	Desert marigold	Showy, yellow daisies on woolly plant
Coreopsis bigelovii	Tickseed	Annual, large golden flowers
Datura meteloides	Sacred datura	Stunning white trumpets, but all plant parts are poisonous
Eriogonum species	Wild buckwheats	Inquire locally for which species to plant
Eschscholzia mexicana	Gold poppy	
Lupinus sparsiflorus	Lupine	Violet; many other species, mostly showy
Martynia species	Devil's claws	Very strange, large, clawed pods
Penstemon eatoni	Firecracker	Tubular scarlet flowers that attract hummingbirds
Penstemon palmeri	Palmer penstemon	Fragrant flowers in pink or lavender
Penstemon parryi	Parry penstemon	Very showy rose flowers
Penstemon pseudospectabilis	Desert penstemon	Pink flowers
Penstemon spectabilis	Penstemon	Lavender-purple, California
Salvia columbariae	Chia	Source of pinole
Stachys coccinea	Scarlet hedge nettle	Scarlet flowers
Zauschneria latifolia	Hummingbird trumpet	More generous of leaf than the California species, but otherwise similar
Zephyranthes longifolia	Zephyr lily	White or pinkish lilies

Eschscholtzia mexicana (**Mexican goldpoppy**) in southwestern semi-desert.

For more information about plants for prairie gardens

Northern Prairie Gardens

Prairie Propagation Handbook, Fifth Edition, by Harold W. Rock. Milwaukee County Park System, Milwaukee, WI. 1977.

Plant descriptions, habitats and propagation techniques for several hundred species of prairie plants.

The Prairie Garden, 70 Native Plants You Can Grow in Town or Country, by J. Robert and B. S. Smith. University of Wisconsin Press, Madison, WI. 1980.

Many of the important wildflowers and grasses are discussed, with illustrations (line drawings and color photographs for each species).

Palouse Prairie Gardens

How to Know the Grasses, Third Edition, by Richard W. Pohl. Wm. C. Brown Co., Dubuque, Iowa. 1978.

An illustrated key with distribution maps. Covers the entire United States. This is perhaps the best book for learning the North American grasses.

High Plains Gardens

Jewels of the Plains, Wildflowers of the Great Plains Grasslands and Hills, by Claude A. Barr. University of Minnesota Press, Minneapolis, MI. 1983.

An extensive encyclopedia of wildflowers of the high plains (Mr. Barr ranged widely in his studies, in New Mexico, Colorado, northern Texas, Oklahoma, Nebraska, and Kansas as well as his native South Dakota); illustrated by color photographs.

The Prairie World, by David Costello. University of Minnesota Press, Minneapolis, MI. 1969.

An illustrated overview of the plant communities of the prairie regions.

Central and Southern Prairie Gardens

Where the Sky Began, Land of the Tallgrass Prairie, by John Madson. Houghton Mifflin, Boston, MA. 1982.

An historical account of what the central third of the United States was like in its pristine state. Contains a 15-page appendix of surviving prairies throughout this region and their exact locations.

Southwestern (Semi-Desert) Grassland Gardens

Desert Plants, Volume 4, Numbers 1-4, 1982. Special Issue: "Biotic Communities of the American Southwest—United States and Mexico." David E. Brown, Editor. University of Arizona, Superior, AZ.

Illustrated guide to plant communities of Arizona, New Mexico, Trans-Pecos Texas, and parts of California, Nevada, and Mexico. Contains lists of plants and animals in all southwestern plant communities.

Shrubland gardens

Shrubland, as described here, includes plant communities of shrubs and small, shrubby trees. In this section, we'll look at native plant gardens based on two of the most common natural landscapes of the West—the shrubby pinyon-juniper woodland of the Southwest and Great Basin, and the chaparral that covers large areas of California.

Gardens patterned after these plant communities can combine attractive, small, evergreen trees, flowering shrubs of all sizes, and brilliant spring wildflowers. Native plants are usually well-adapted to poor soils, drought, and high summer temperatures, suiting them for difficult sites where little else will grow.

Design

Shrubland and woodland communities contain various plant habitats. Some plants are found in full, hot sun on a south-facing slope; others grow in moist woodlands on the cooler north slopes. Learn the requirements of each plant, and design your garden to place plants with similar needs together to simplify maintenance.

Note the way different vegetation types merge in the shrubland and woodland. Pattern your garden after the natural communities by planting a more lush woodland in the canyons and on north-facing slopes, drought-tolerant shrubs in hot, open areas, and islands of taller trees and moisture-loving shrubs in areas that are naturally wet.

Many shrubland plants flower in spring and summer. Others have bright berries or an attractive branching pattern in winter. Choose the plants for your garden to give a long season of bloom and visual interest, and arrange them in massed plantings for the best effect. Many shrubland plants have characteristically scented foliage, and should be placed by a path where the leaves can be rubbed and pinched to release their fragrance.

Grasses grow with the shrubs and trees among the chaparral, in open glades or on warm slopes and hilltops. In California, these are mostly introduced annual grasses, which have replaced the native perennial grasses; in the Southwest, they are the native wheatgrasses, gramas, and others. Open grassy areas in your garden

California's coastal chaparral is home to most of the plants used in this garden. From lower right are Arctostaphyllos hookeri, *a mound of lavender-flowered lupine, and banks of blue* Ceonothus impressus.

are ideal places for a display of bright annual wildflowers. The flowers can be seeded by one of the techniques recommended in the section on meadow gardens (above) and the area mowed following spring bloom to keep it from becoming unsightly.

Group the plants together in "islands" to minimize maintenance and create attractive displays. The islands can be quite large—40 feet or more in length, and 20 feet or more in width—with wide paths of gravel or wood chips between. Place the tallest shrubs or trees at the center of the island, with lower, spreading shrubs near the outer edges. Mound the soil on the island slightly for good drainage. Space the plants widely to allow them room to grow to their mature size, so that they can mine a large soil area for water and nutrients.

To provide a place for the more dwarf, spreading shrubs and perennials, consider including a rock garden area in your shrubland landscape. If your garden is large, the small trees of the woodlands will add shade and provide a habitat for those shrubs that grow in the understory. If your garden is small, use tall shrubs instead of trees. Many shrubs can grow to 15 or 20 feet.

Soil preparation

In areas of existing grassland, you will need first to control the annual grasses and germinate the weed seeds in the soil by keeping it moist for several weeks. Kill the seedlings as they germinate with an herbicide or shallow cultivation. In California, or other areas with a weather pattern of summer drought, you will have to germinate weeds in the fall and spring. Many weed seeds will only germinate in the cooler weather of fall (October is best) or as the soil warms in spring.

Most chaparral plants grow on thin, rocky, upland soils, and do not tolerate the heavy, water-holding clays of the lowlands. If your soil is heavy, you can improve its drainage by incorporating large amounts of organic materials into the top several inches. Composted sawdust and other treated wood products are excellent amendments, but avoid manure, which can cause root diseases in some chaparral plants. You can also improve your soil by digging a wide planting hole for each plant (not deeper than the plant's rootball), refilling much of it with the now-loosened native soil, and adding organic amendments to the remaining backfill soil that is packed around the roots. Don't add more than one part of organic material to three parts native soil; a richer mix than this can discourage the plant from ever extending its roots beyond the backfill.

Avoid pulling extra soil up around existing trees or shrubs in your garden. Many shrubland and western

California poppies dominate this California shrubland planting. The yellow-flowered shrub in the upper right is Fremontodendron californicum. *Modern hybrids of this showy bloomer have prolonged blooming seasons.*

woodland natives are sensitive to soil around their trunks, and within a few years may decline and die as a result. Mistakes of this kind are often made when building a home among large, established native trees.

Some natives of the foothill chaparral areas prefer a slightly acidic soil, though most do quite well with the neutral or slightly alkaline soils prevalent in these regions.

Planting and seeding

Many shrubland natives are available as seedlings or container plants. Because their seeds can have complex dormancy patterns that require several treatments to overcome, buying plants can be an easier way to get the garden started.

Begin by planting any trees so they'll get an early start, then follow with the most important groups of shrubs. If you will be propagating any plants from seed or cuttings, start them early as well. The best planting time in these warm-summer regions is in fall, just before the rains begin. Over the winter, the young plants can develop large root systems, readying them for rapid growth in spring.

The large planting holes mentioned above should be at least 16 inches in diameter for a standard one-gallon container plant that is planted

in an open area. Under trees, the hole should be a couple of feet wide. This will remove tree roots and give the new plants a chance to compete with the trees. Around each new plant, build a watering basin. This is a low wall of earth a foot or more out from the plant, to hold water near the roots. Break a hole in the wall to let it drain during the winter, then rebuild it in spring. Some species are especially sensitive to excess moisture in their root zone and need to be planted on a slight mound to provide the drainage they need.

If you wish, you can add to the planting hole one or more tablets of a time-released fertilizer. This will get the young plant off to a good start. Some of these products can supply nutrients to the plant for more than a year. Mulch all new plantings with several inches of wood chips or other organic materials, but keep the mulch away from the stems of woody plants.

Some native shrubland species, especially annual wildflowers, can be easily started from seed. The best sowing time is in fall or summer, just before the rains are expected. Sow the large seeds first. These seeds need a slight covering of soil, so rake them in lightly. Then sow the small seeds, and lightly water everything you've sown. Keep the area moist during the

germination period (several weeks to several months).

Maintenance

In these areas of periodic drought and high seasonal temperatures, you'll need to water your new plants frequently during their first season of growth—up to once or twice a week, depending on the weather. Begin right after planting if the rains don't come as expected. The second season, you can probably taper off to once a month for the most drought-tolerant plants. Once every month or two will be adequate in succeeding seasons. When they are established in the landscape, you can let many of the hardiest chaparral natives go without water all summer, but most will look better with occasional watering.

Some chaparral natives are from cooler coastal areas. If you plant these species farther inland, they may require biweekly watering even when mature. Be sure not to plant coastal species near the tougher plants from inland regions, as excessive summer water can kill the inland natives. When watering, always fill the watering basin several times to get water deep into the soil. This will encourage deep rooting, and the plants will be more tolerant of drought as a result. If your garden is large, you may wish to install a water-conserving drip irrigation system to do the watering.

Keep a mulch around the plants to retain water in the soil and discourage weeds. Pre-emergent herbicides will also help to discourage weeds; applied under the mulch, they make it more effective.

Don't be discouraged if your chaparral plants look dry during summer and early fall. They will revive with the winter rains. Chaparral plants (and plants from other hot regions) make most of their growth in fall and spring, essentially ceasing growth during the hot summer. Some will drop many of their leaves as hot weather arrives. This is their way of lightening the burden of leaves that must be maintained through the difficult dry season.

Most shrubland plants will require no fertilization after planting. Some woodland natives may benefit from occasional fertilization, but the needs of almost all shrubland plants will be supplied by an organic mulch, which slowly feeds nutrients to the soil.

Plants for shrubland gardens
Chaparral and Oak Woodland

Trees

Acer macrophyllum	Big-leaf maple	Fast-growing; to 100 feet
Arbutus menziesii	Madrone	Red bark and berries
Lyonothamnus floribundus var. *asplenifolius*	Catalina ironwood	Fernlike foliage, shaggy bark
Pinus coulteri	Coulter pine	Large dark blue-green cones
Pinus sabiniana	Grey pine	Gray; drought-resistant; edible seeds
Prunus ilicifolia	Holly-leaved cherry	Small evergreen tree, large shrub
Prunus lyonii	Catalina cherry	Evergreen; dark green narrowly ovate leaves
Quercus agrifolia	Coast live oak	Evergreen, gnarled
Quercus douglasii	Blue oak	Leaves blue-green
Quercus lobata	Valley oak	Large, deciduous
Umbellularia californica	California bay	Leaves can be substituted for bay leaves in cooking

Shrubs

Arctostaphylos species and cultivars	Manzanita	Many species in cultivation
Baccharis pilularis and cultivars	Dwarf coyote bush	Excellent ground cover
Carpenteria californica	Carpenteria	Needs some shade; showy white flowers
Ceanothus species	California lilacs	Showy ground covers and shrubs
Dendromecon rigida subspecies *harfordii*	Island bush poppy	Flowers yellow; needs sandy soil
Eriogonum arborescens	Santa Cruz Island buckwheat	Drought resistant
Eriogonum giganteum	St.-Catherine's-lace	Used in dried flower arrangements
Fremontodendron californicum	Flannel bush	Showy yellow flowers; needs perfect drainage
Garrya elliptica	Silk-tassel bush	Ornamentals flowering in late winter and early spring
Heteromeles arbutifolia	Toyon	Evergreen; red berries are important winter bird food
Mimulus aurantiacus	Monkeyflower	Yellow flowers throughout the year
Rhamnus californica	Coffeeberry	To 6 feet; evergreen; understory species
Rhamnus crocea	Redberry	To 3 feet; evergreen; bright red fruit
Ribes viburnifolium	Catalina currant	Adaptable as ground cover; in shade under oaks
Salvia clevelandii	Sage	Leaves can be substituted for culinary sage

Forbs

Clarkia biloba	Clarkia	Notched petals; needs sun
Dodecatheon clevelandii and *D. hendersonii*	Shooting star	Flowers of white, magenta, lavender, or purple
Eschscholzia californica	California poppy	California state flower
Fritillaria lanceolata	Checker lily	Light shade; many ricelike bulblets
Iris douglasiana	Wild iris	Flowers from shades of purple to cream or white
Lupinus nanus	Lupine	Most California lupines are showy
Romneya coulteri	Matilija poppy	Very large and showy; grow in canyons in nature, but adapt well to cultivation
Zauschneria californica	California fuchsia	Red flowers in late summer and fall

Pinyon-Juniper Woodland

Pinyon-juniper woodland is dominated by species of pines and junipers which, though similar, change somewhat from state to state. Consult your local nursery or department of botany to see which species are native to your area. Pinyons and junipers should be widely spaced so that the shrubs and forbs that grow among them receive the sunlight they need. All the plants of the appropriate grassland lists can be grown in the sunniest spots of a pinyon-juniper planting.

Trees

Pinus species *cembroides, monophylla,* and *quadrifolia*	Pinyon pine	Cones produce edible nuts
Juniperus species *californica, deppeana, monosperma, osteosperma,* and *scopulorum*	Junipers	Plants fragrant, becoming gnarled; bright berries
Acer glabrum	Rocky Mountain maple	Scarlet fall color; shrub or small tree

Shrubs

Artemisia tridentata	Big sagebrush	Soft, grey foliage
Cercocarpus species *intricatus, ledifolius,* and *montanus*	Mountain mahogany	Shrub or low tree; subtle
Cowania mexicana	Cliff rose	White to yellow flowers
Crysothamnus nauseosus	Rabbitbrush	Whitish, showy yellow flowers
Fallugia paradoxa	Apache plume	Feathery seedheads
Fendlera rupicola	Fendler's bush	Waxy white 2-inch blooms
Opuntia imbricata	Cane cactus	Red flowers and yellow fruits
Purshia tridentata	Antelope bitterbrush	
Quercus gambeli	Gambel's oak	White oak; gold fall color
Shepherdia argentea	Silver buffalo berry	To 18 feet; thorny; edible fruits
Yucca baccata	Banana yucca	Some shade; creamy flowers tinged with purple
Yucca glauca	Great Plains yucca	Requires full sun; greenish-cream flowers
Yucca schottii	Schott's yucca	Small, white flowers; to 15 feet

(continued next page)

The western redbud (Cercis occidentalis) *blooms behind a border of Oregon grape and other shrubs. They serve as a transition to the tall pine woods behind them.*

Forbs

Castilleja integra	Indian paintbrush	Showy red leaves resembling flowers at branch tips
Corydalis aurea	Golden smoke	Like a yellow Dutchman's breeches
Coryphantha vivipara	Pincushion cactus	Pink flowers; to 6 inches
Echinocereus fendleri	Hedgehog cactus	Purple flowers; to 18 inches
Echinocereus pectinatus	Arizona rainbow cactus	Red or pink flowers
Echinocereus triglochidiatus	Claret cup	Large scarlet flowers
Echinocereus viridiflorus	Green-flowered hedgehog	Subtle; yellow-green flowers
Gilia aggregata	Fairy trumpet	Scarlet; attracts hummingbirds
Helianthus annuus	Common sunflower	To 10 feet; edible seeds
Hymenoxys argentea	Hymenoxys	Silvery dwarf "sunflower"
Lesquerella species *arizonica* and *intermedia*	Bladder-pod	Yellow flowers
Liatris punctata	Blazing-star	Purple; fall bloomer
Penstemon barbatus	Scarlet bugler	Attract hummingbirds
Phlox nana	Canyon phlox	Large, deep pink flowers
Psilostrophe tagetina	Paperflower	Yellow; good for dried floral arrangements
Thermopsis montana	Golden banner	Similar to lupine in form
Townsendia exscapa	Easter daisy	"Easter basket" of white daisies, often tinged with pink or purple
Zinnia grandiflora	Wild zinnia	Yellow; looks nothing like a garden zinnia

For more information about plants for shrubland gardens

Chaparral Gardens

Growing California Native Plants, by Marjorie G. Schmidt. University of California Press, Berkeley CA. 1980.

Information on growing trees, shrubs, and herbs native to California. Author has extensive personal experience with growing this flora.

A California Flora, by Phillip A. Munz and David D. Keck. University of California Press, Berkeley CA. 1959.

The classic text for identifying California plants. Dr. Munz also wrote a series of popular paperbacks on California plants (California Mountain Wildflowers, California Desert Wildflowers, etc.), which are also in print.

See also Western Coastal Gardens

Pinyon Juniper Woodland Gardens

Arizona Flora, by Thomas H. Kearney and Robert H. Peebles. Second Edition with supplement by John Thomas Howell, Elizabeth McClintock, and collaborators. University of California Press, Berkeley and Los Angeles, CA.

The classic flora for Arizona. This volume is affordable and lists most of the species which occur in New Mexico, for which no affordable flora is available.

Desert gardens

The deserts of the western United States include several diverse areas: the cold sagebrush desert of the Great Basin, the Mojave of Southern California, and the warmer Sonoran Desert of Arizona and Chihuahuan Desert of New Mexico and Texas. Although temperature extremes and the timing of the rainy season may differ from one area to another, all these desert regions have several things in common: brilliant sunlight, high soil and air temperatures, and low soil moisture levels.

These characteristics, in addition to difficult soils and strong winds, make the desert a difficult growing environment for plants, especially those introduced from milder climates. Trying to grow these exotic plants in the desert can make gardening seem like a battle against nature. You can avoid much of the battle by selecting and planting the native desert plants of your region in your garden. These species have adapted to the growing conditions of your area over the centuries; not only will your garden be less work with natives, it will be visually appropriate to your region.

Design

Plan a garden to meet your family's needs, and to match plants to the habitats of your site. Begin the design process with a careful site analysis, especially noting the site microclimates—the extremes of bright sunlight, glare, and winter winds. Design your plantings to minimize these problems with sun screens, windbreaks, and shade trees. Note also any areas of difficult soil, such as spots where the soil is shallow, saline, or alkaline. You'll need to improve soil conditions in these areas for plants to grow.

Learn about the plant communities in your local area. Your native desert plants may be those of the low desert, the desert grassland, the sagebrush community, or other desert plant environments. Use your area's native plants as the mainstay of your garden design. You can also borrow the natives of nearby regions, especially those of higher altitude, such as the plants of the pinyon-juniper woodland or other low-elevation groups of the Rocky Mountain forest. These plants can create a more lush, "oasis" effect near the house or patio,

but they will need more water than the true desert natives.

Do not feel that you have to cover every inch of ground with plants in a desert garden. Typical desert vegetation only covers about 25 percent of the ground in many areas. Concentrate your plants in "island" plantings, where they're needed for landscape effect.

Desert natives need not be restricted to informal gardens of flowing lines and asymmetrical shapes. Many of the native shrubs can be used in hedges, or as backgrounds for formal flower beds, and desert trees can border the garden neatly or shade an elegant patio. Desert wildflowers can play a role in both a flower border and an open meadow.

Some possible components of your desert garden are a shady patio, islands of desert shrubs and trees, a dry wash to suggest the arroyos of the desert, a small fountain or trickle of water, and a meadow or open field of native grasses and wildflowers.

Soil preparation

To help conserve water in the finished landscape, grade the soil before planting to channel runoff from roofs and paving into the planting areas. This will satisfy the needs of many hardy plants for supplemental watering.

Once any grading is done, begin to work with your soil. Any areas that

have fairly deep soil and are only mildly alkaline will need little improvement beyond standard planting techniques. Many desert gardens may inherit more difficult soils, however: these may be high in soluble salts, or have concentrated areas of sodic soils or the impermeable soil layer called *caliche*.

Desert soils are frequently high in salts, because these natural products of rock weathering are not washed deep into the soil as they would be in areas of higher rainfall, but concentrate near the surface. From here they are taken up by plant roots and can burn the plant's leaves or stunt its growth. A soil test or information from your county extension agent can help you learn whether your soils are *saline* (as such soils are called), and how to counteract them. The usual treatment for saline soils is to water very heavily at the time of planting and again several times during each year. This is called "leaching," and will usually wash the salts out of the surface soil.

Sodic soils are those high in sodium salts. Because of its chemical properties, sodium destroys soil texture, creating a soil with an impervious surface that slows water drainage almost to a standstill. Very few plants will grow in these soils. The remedy is to replace the sodium in the soil with calcium, which creates a more open structure; this can be done in

Two blooming desert trees adorn this garden: paloverde is on the left, and cat's claw acacia on the right.

The area outside the walled garden is "saved vegetation," carefully preserved desert landscape. The area within the wall is saved for less rugged (and less prickly) specimens.

several ways. If your soil also has a layer of caliche, which is a form of calcium, it can be broken down to liberate calcium to the soil by treating with iron sulfate or sulfur. (Be careful with iron sulfate: it stains concrete and rocks.) If caliche is not present, gypsum applied to the soil surface and lightly worked in will provide calcium. Get specific advice on your soils and their treatment from your county extension agent.

Caliche is a concentration of limestone that forms a cementlike layer in the soil. This layer may be just a few inches or several feet below the surface, but it absolutely stops water drainage and root penetration. The best treatment is a physical one—break it up, with a backhoe or a pick. You needn't do this in your whole yard, only in areas where you'll be planting, or in holes dug for individual plants. If the caliche is too deep to remove, be sure that each hole will drain when filled with water.

Native desert plants are usually more tolerant of soil problems than exotic species. Even so, most natives will benefit from being planted in large planting holes, with about 30 percent organic matter such as peat, manure, or nitrified sawdust added to the backfill soil around the roots. Or plant them on mounds of improved soil placed on the native soil.

Organic mulches are a good long-term soil improvement strategy. Spread mulch several inches deep around new plants and replace it periodically, to feed the soil and keep the surface from crusting due to heat and rain. Use fibrous mulches rather than fine materials in windy areas, or cover finer materials with a layer of crushed rock or gravel.

Climate control

To make your garden a pleasant retreat, you will need to soften the harshest aspects of your desert climate—winds, sun, and glare.

Desert winds can be quite strong in some areas, especially if your home is built right in the desert, unprotected by adjacent houses. Here there is nothing to stop the wind's drying influence. Your best protection, if you have room for it, may be a windbreak of mixed trees and shrubs. Because a windbreak slows the air flow, it can create a pocket of higher humidity behind it, benefitting the plants that grow there. Stone walls, fences, and overhead structures can also provide shelter and make the garden a better growing environment.

Lessen the sun's heat by planting deciduous shade trees, especially on the south and west sides of the house, and above paved areas. If glare is a problem, plant ground covers, shrubs, and trees to intercept it.

Planting

Planting out seedlings is the easiest way to establish a desert garden. Sowing seed directly outdoors will often be only frustrating, requiring almost constant attention to keep the seed and seedbed moist. However, you may have to grow seedlings of many desert natives, especially in the Great Basin region, because many are not available as plants. You may even have to collect seed and cuttings from nature and do your own propagation, in order to grow many of the finest native desert plants.

If the seed of a species is available and inexpensive, you may want to sow it directly on a prepared seedbed outdoors. Sow in fall, winter, or early spring. If the seed is expensive or rare, pretreat it during the winter (by stratification or scarification as appropriate), then sow it in early spring in flats. Move the seedlings to 2-inch containers as they grow, and keep them in pots until they are several inches tall. Plant them in the garden in late summer or fall.

When planting a garden with seedlings and container plants, bear in mind that the smaller sizes—especially plants in 2-inch pots and 1-gallon containers—will be easiest to establish, although they must be protected from wind and heat.

Dig large holes for transplants—at least twice the diameter of the rootball, and larger in poorer soils. If water does not drain readily from the hole, dig a drainage "chimney" at the bottom of the hole, about 6 inches in diameter by several feet deep. Refill the hole most of the way with the pulverized native soil. Add tablets or granules of a time-released fertilizer to the backfill. Loosen some of the native soil at the edge of the hole and blend it with the improved backfill to make a transition zone to native soil. This transition zone encourages roots to grow into the native soil.

Plant young seedlings or container plants in fall or early spring. Do not let the roots dry out before planting. Plant promptly after bringing the plants home, or keep them in the shade and well-watered.

Other garden materials
Other materials that go well with desert plants include railroad ties for raised beds or walls, adobe bricks or rough-cut cedar for fencing, and cobblestones for creating dry washes. Shredded bark makes a useful and attractive mulch that won't blow away in the wind. *Crusher fines* (known in some areas as decomposed granite or ½-minus, indicating its size) make a good utility path when watered and rolled. Red cinder rock can be used as a mulch to provide color contrast to the landscape.

Water management
Conserve water in your garden by placing plants with similar water needs together. Not all desert plants are of the drought-tolerant, water-hoarding sort. Some grow in nature along desert washes, or in seeps or wet spots where their roots can reach water. These plants will need a similarly moist spot in the garden, or regular watering.

Another type of plant could be called drought-avoiding. These are the annual flowers that spring up in the moist soil after rains, and complete their life cycles before dry weather returns. These species will need little extra watering in the garden, and can be planted in dry spots.

The third type of desert plant is the genuine *xerophyte*, a plant that grows quite well in hot, dry conditions. This group of plants includes the largest number of desert natives, plants that have evolved mechanisms for efficiently extracting any available water from the soil, and relinquishing it only very slowly. These species can be planted together in the more distant areas of your garden and left on their own without supplemental watering after a few years.

Don't be afraid of bare space in your desert garden. It is typical in natural deserts; if unwatered, it will sprout few weeds. Spring bloom of Encina *(bitterbrush) steals the show here; later, the architectural forms of cactus will be most obvious.*

Space your desert plants widely in the landscape. This conserves water by giving each plant room to spread its roots through a large volume of soil. Placing several inches of an organic or stone mulch around plants will also help conserve moisture by slowing evaporation from the soil.

Because you will be watering the thirsty natives of arroyo, seepage areas, and mountain foothills most frequently, plant them near the house where they will be easiest to care for. Another reason to have these plants near the house is that they are often the most lush-looking plants in the desert, and can be used to create a verdant, oasis landscape surrounding the patio, entry, and living areas. These parts of the garden may need watering as often as once a week during hot weather, even after they are established, and will need some watering right through winter.

Plant the drought-hardy natives of the desert lowlands in the farther reaches of the garden, where they will blend your created landscape into any surrounding natural vegetation. These plants will need extra care and watering for their first few seasons in the garden.

Nearly all desert plants will benefit from some supplemental watering during periods of drought. Extra watering will also be helpful when the weather is especially hot and dry. Remember to soak plants deeply when you water.

Plan to leach accumulated salts from the soil around your plants by deep flooding several times a year, first in early spring, then periodically throughout the growing season. Installation of a drip irrigation system can greatly simplify your watering labors, and will prevent water waste by putting the water right where it is needed in the landscape.

Other maintenance
After planting, desert natives will rarely need fertilization. Occasionally, some species may turn yellow, especially in early spring; spray these with chelated iron. Plants in areas receiving frequent watering may also need extra fertilization. An annual application of a balanced lawn and garden fertilizer will make up for the nutrients leached from the soils.

Some desert trees send up great numbers of sucker shoots from their base when young. Remove these in summer. Wildflowers and shrubs that bloom heavily will look better and bloom longer if clipped back after their first bloom. If your desert garden includes a wildflower and grass meadow, mow it once a year between November and January, leaving the cuttings on the ground as mulch.

Opuntia violacea var. macrocentra. ***Bright yellow flowers with red centers fade to rose. Opuntias do well on exposed rocky banks.***

Plants for desert gardens
Great Basin
The following list covers shrubs and wildflowers of the basin floor and foothills. Mountain "islands" of higher elevations in the Great Basin support a pinyon-juniper forest, with forests similar to Rocky Mountain flora at the highest elevations.

Shrubs

Artemisia tridentata	Big sagebrush	Gray; abundant
Chrysothamnus nauseosus	Rabbit brush	Gray; showy yellow flower clusters in autumn
Cowania mexicana	Cliff rose	Dry slopes
Ephedra viridis	Mormon tea	Green "stick plants"
Fallugia paradoxa	Apache plume	White flowers; fluffy seed heads
Haplopappus acaulis	Haplopappus	Yellow "daisies" on shrubby mats
Holodiscus boursieri	Ocean spray	Dry rocky slopes
Peraphyllum ramosissimum	Shrub of rose family	Desert washes
Purshia tridentata	Bitterbrush	To 10 feet
Shepherdia argentea	Buffalo berry	Needs moisture

Forbs

Allium anceps	Wild onion	Rose flowers with purple midveins
Astragalus pterocarpus	Winged seed milk vetch	Flowers purple or white
Astragalus purshii	Pursh's milk vetch	Woolly pods
Baileya multiradiata	Desert marigold	Very showy
Balsamorhiza sagittata	Arrow-leafed balsamroot	Yellow "daisies"
Cymopterus globosus	Cymopterus	Ground-hugging herb in parsley family
Delphinium andersonii	Anderson's larkspur	Grows with sagebrush
Erigeron species	Daisies	Flowers white or lavender
Eriogonum caespitosum	Wild buckwheat	Flowers white, pink, or blue
Eriogonum umbellatum	Sulphur flower	Variable in the basin
Eschscholzia californica	California poppy	Orange flowers
Fritillaria pudica	Yellow bells	Nodding bells in spring
Ipomopsis (Gilia) aggregata	Fairy trumpet	Tubular bells
Lewisia brachycalyx	Lewisia	Needs moisture in spring
Lewisia nevadensis	Lewisia	Moisture in spring, dry in summer
Penstemon palmeri	Palmer penstemon	Large pink flowers
Penstemon rubicundus	Penstemon	Showy pink blooms
Penstemon speciosus	Showy penstemon	Large blue flowers
Zauschneria californica latifolia	California fuchsia	Showy scarlet flowers; attract hummingbirds

Deserts
Warm Deserts

We combine here the floras of the Southwest deserts. The floras of these deserts are distinctive and many species do not occur in all of them. However, because of space limitation, it was necessary to pool these communities. Inquire locally for information about which species are native to your area if you wish to plant only local native species. Also, suitable grasses and forbs are given in the Southwestern Grassland list.

Trees

Bursera fagaroides	Elephant tree	Resin of this smooth-barked tree was burned as incense in Mayan and Aztec temples; very gnarled and mysterious
Cercidium floridum and C. *microphyllum*	Paloverde	Bright green trunks and branches
Lysiloma thornberi	Desert lacetree	Spectacular; shrub or small tree
Olneya tesota	Desert ironwood	Handsome flowers; to 25 feet
Washingtonia filifera	California palm	Beautiful; looks tropical
Yucca brevifolia	Joshua tree	Famous arborescent species

Shrubs

Beloperone californica	Chuparosa	Red flowers that attract hummingbirds
Cassia covesii and C. *lindheimerana*	Desert senna	Yellow flowers
Chilopsis linearis	Desert catalpa	Attractive flowers; catalpalike pendant pods
Dalea greggii	Indigo bush	Showy rose-purple flowers
Encelia farinosa	Brittlebush	Gum was used as incense in Baja California churches
Erythrina flabelliformis	Coral bean	Showy red flowers; scarlet poisonous beans used for necklaces in Mexico
Fouquieria splendens	Ocotillo	Spiny desert shrub; showy flowers
Simmondsia chinensis	Jojoba	"Beans" yield a high-quality oil
Sophora arizonica	Arizona mountain laurel	Flowers like wisteria
Tecoma stans	Yellow trumpetbush	Widely in cultivation; used for browse by bighorn sheep

Stem Succulents

Agave palmeri	Palmer century plant	Large and majestic
Agave parryi	Parry century plant	Similar to *A. palmeri*
Agave parviflora	Century plant	Very small and modest
Dasylirion species including D. *wheeleri*	Sotol	Large and showy
Yucca elata	Palmilla	Showy; widely-planted; increases in overgrazed rangeland
Yucca schidigera	Yucca	Leaves like *Y. baccata*, but somewhat arborescent

Cacti

Learning our desert cacti is a project in itself. Many species have small natural ranges. Beyond the few widespread species listed below, you should consult local nurseries and manuals for additional local species.

Carnegiea gigantea	Saguaro	Arizona state flower
Ferocactus species, especially *F. acanthodes, covillei,* and *wislizeni*	Barrel cactus	Large and showy
Lemaireocereus thurberi	Organpipe cactus	Branches from base; pink flowers
Mammillaria species	Pincushion cacti	Many desert natives; consult local manuals
Opuntia species	Prickly pear	Flowers yellow, white, or magenta
Peniocereus greggii	Queen-of-the-night	Fragrant, white flowers bloom in evening and wither by morning

For more information about plants for desert gardens

Great Basin Gardens

The New York Botanical Garden is currently publishing a multivolume flora of the Intermountain Region (Nevada, Utah and parts of several adjacent states) entitled **Intermountain Flora.** This flora is very expensive but should be available in libraries. Three volumes have been published so far.

Warm Desert Gardens

See also Southwestern (Semi-Desert) Grassland.

Cacti of the United States and Canada, by Lyman Benson. Stanford University Press, Stanford, CA. 1983.

Comprehensive, expensive, and available in libraries. Other books by Lyman Benson on cacti, such as The Cacti of Arizona *are also worth tracking down.*

Desert Wild Flowers, by Edmund C. Jaeger. Stanford University Press, Stanford, CA. 1969.

An illustrated flora of common desert forbs.

Right: Agave parryi.

When planning a rock garden, keep small treasures down front where they can be appreciated, tall showy flowers in less accessible places. This Boston area rock garden artfully imitates nature's random patterns.

Rock gardens

Rock gardens are usually built to display small alpine plants and other dwarf shrubs and perennials. Many of the finest North American native plants are ideal rock garden plants; these include the truly alpine plants of the high mountains, the sun-loving wildflowers of the Great Plains and the seashore, and low-growing shrubs from many regions. For the shady rock garden, many of the smallest woodland wildflowers and ferns are beautiful choices.

The plant lists for this section concentrate on plants for sunny rock gardens. Those seeking plant ideas for a shaded rockery will find many possibilities among the wildflowers listed under Forest Gardens.

Design

A rock garden is most attractive if it appears natural, a part of the site rather than something artificially created. Begin designing your rock garden by exploring mountainous areas near you. Notice how the rock formations are arranged, where soil accumulates around the individual rocks, and where the small plants find growing places among them. In some areas, you can find hilly landscapes with rocks at low elevations, but you can learn the most by visiting high altitude alpine areas.

Select a site for the rock garden carefully. In cool areas, the site should be in full sun; in dry-summer areas, however, the garden will benefit from afternoon shade and should avoid southern or western exposures. If you use trees for shade, they should be far enough away that their roots won't penetrate the rock garden.

A rock garden does not require a hill or slope, though it may look most at home there. If you have a large property in its natural state, there may be ledges or rock outcrops that will be perfect for rock plants; in this case you can plant several small rock gardens in these spots, interspersed with other garden plantings. You could also design a single, larger rock garden on a slope, above a stone wall, or on flat ground. In a garden that includes stone walls or terraces, you can grow rock plants in the wall crevices as well as draping over the stones from above.

Any large rock garden will need paths, or steps if it is on a slope. In a garden on flat land, paths can imitate nature as they wend their way through slightly mounded plantings (mounding can also be suggested by the skillful combination of larger and smaller plants). On the paths themselves, you can grow rock plants in wide cracks between the paving stones, or in more formal borders.

After choosing the site and roughly conceiving the type of rock garden you want, take time to visualize it. Much of the design of small gardens can be worked out in the garden by careful visualization and experimentation with topography, stone placement, and plants.

Plan to center the garden on a number of large stones—the largest ones you can handle with the help of friends or available power equipment. Fit these large stones into the landscape first, then work smaller stones into the pattern.

Rock and water naturally go together. If you have a stream or pool already in the garden, or can construct one, it will be a natural complement to the rock garden.

When selecting plants, learn the soil, water, and sun exposure needs of each, and group plants with similar requirements in the different areas of the garden. Those of true alpine origin will need an open, gritty soil and some summer watering in dry-summer areas. The wildflowers and dwarf plants of lower elevations will usually do best in heavier soils, and may need some summer drought.

Place plants according to their growth rates, too, putting together those that grow slowly, and planting well away from these any plants that grow rapidly and can be invasive. Rock gardens can easily be dominated by a few aggressive species if this segregation is not practiced.

Design the garden with ample space between plants. Learn about the potential size of each species and give it that much room and more. Open spaces in the rock garden, mulched with stone chips or gravel, can look

perfectly natural since this is the character of many alpine areas. In fact, *scree* (steep slopes of loose rocks that accumulate at the base of cliffs or are left behind by glaciers) are a common alpine habitat.

Site preparation and construction

Early weed control is essential to your rock garden's success. Persistent invasive weeds can be the bane of your gardening hours, so get rid of them before planting. Kill them with a systemic herbicide. If the soil is filled with weed seeds, germinate them by keeping the soil moist for a few weeks and kill the seedlings as they appear with an herbicide or shallow cultivation.

Choosing stones for your garden is an important job. Ideally, the stones should come from nearby, and should be of one rock type. For walls and terraces, you'll want smaller stones, either flat or rounded; for paths, use flat stones; and, as the backbone of the garden, select several large boulders. The garden need not be jammed with rocks. As you collect or purchase the rocks for your garden, favor the larger sizes; even the largest stones, when half-buried in soil to look natural, can seem to shrink remarkably.

You can build a rock wall with or without mortar. A dry-laid wall (one without mortar) looks the most natural and permits you to plant in the crevices between stones. A mortared wall may be stronger, and can be as attractive as a dry-laid wall if the mortar joints are hidden and plants are trained to grow over it from above. A low wall needs no foundation; a wall taller than two or three feet should be set on a concrete footing extending the length of the wall and 12 to 18 inches below the ground. Set the largest stones toward the bottom of the wall, the smallest on top. If you are building with flat stones, slope each one downward from the front to the back of the wall, so rain will flow toward the plant roots in the crevices.

If the slope above the wall is wet or poorly drained, lay drain line at the base of the wall on the back side. Surround it with a bed of several inches of river rock or drain gravel, and install enough drain line to carry the water to a lower point in the garden, or to a gravel-filled pit.

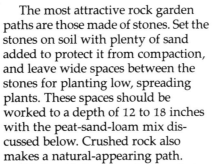

Small rock plants can be inserted into an already completed dry rock wall using fine tools like this chopstick. They will be watered by seepage from the slope behind, but will never be in stagnant, soggy soil, which they would not tolerate.

The most attractive rock garden paths are those made of stones. Set the stones on soil with plenty of sand added to protect it from compaction, and leave wide spaces between the stones for planting low, spreading plants. These spaces should be worked to a depth of 12 to 18 inches with the peat-sand-loam mix discussed below. Crushed rock also makes a natural-appearing path.

Work with large boulders only in dry, warm weather. Handle them carefully to avoid injuring yourself. It helps to have some muscular friends, a large handtruck, and some stout 2-inch-thick boards on hand. Position each boulder as it was in nature; if it is on a hill, be sure it is well-supported by soil or buried rubble. Try to form an irregular, subtle composition of the large stones. You may want to return to the mountains at this time for inspiration, or visit a nearby Japanese garden. The final step in preparing the site is to add the small stones.

Soil and drainage

Most rock garden plants come from alpine areas, where they have evolved their dwarf forms in response to snow, winds, and a very short growing season. Soils in these areas are usually loose and porous, and drain rapidly. The soils are often rocky, and humus content is usually low. If you are growing true alpine plants in your rock garden, you must match these conditions. Any species of small lowland plants you add to the garden can be set in sections that have somewhat heavier soil.

Many garden soils have a high clay content and are not suitable for a rock garden. If your soils are heavy, you may need to remove them to a depth of 12 to 18 inches or more and refill the area with a specially prepared soil mix. If your soils are lighter, you may be able to add sand and peat to the native soil and plant in it. Check your soil's texture by squeezing a small, damp clod of it in your hand. Open your hand and prod the clod with your finger. If it breaks apart easily, the soil is adequate for most rock gardens. If the clod is difficult to break, or only dents at a prod, the clay content is too high.

A good soil mix for most rock garden plants is 1 part weed-free garden loam, 1 part sphagnum peat, and 1 part river sand. If the loam has some clay content, add more sand and peat. To insure that the soil will have rapid drainage, some rock gardeners recommend installing drainage pipes beneath the soil in particularly wet situations. Be sure that any water collected by the drain line is drained away from the rock garden.

If you are growing mostly forest plants in a shaded rock garden, your soil mix should be closer to the character of forest soils—darker and richer in humus than the soils of other rock gardens. If you are growing true alpines, you may need to locate a gravelly soil similar to that found on mountaintops. Alpines are frequently found in a gritty soil with the water table just under the surface. Note the soil preferences of the individual plants, and amend the soil to match.

Planting

In choosing plants, bear in mind than many alpine species are fairly easy to grow; begin your garden with these. Later, you will probably want to experiment with some of the more elegant and difficult species. These plants will require you to have a more exact knowledge of their native habitat, may need a special planting mix, and will have very specific moisture preferences. For your trouble, they can reward you with beautiful form and texture, and unique blooms.

Many native rock garden plants are available from specialty nurseries throughout the country. Most are sold as young seedlings or in small containers. This small size can make it easier to plant them in tight places. Dwarf conifer species and shrubs may be available in large containers or balled-and-burlapped. Planting a few such large specimens can give a visual lift to a young rock garden. Dig large planting holes, and be sure that drainage is good.

The best planting time for rock garden species varies from region to region. Generally, early fall and spring are good, because the new plants will not be immediately stressed by severe weather.

Leave a small watering basin around each new plant, and water it thoroughly as it is planted. Water frequently during the first few weeks after planting if the weather is hot. Finish the planting with a mulch of stone chips or gravel.

When building a dry-laid rock wall, set wall plants into the wall as you go. Firm the soil around them, and be careful not to damage them during the remainder of the job.

Maintenance

Weeding of the rock garden must usually be done by hand, and must be done regularly. Good weed control during the preparative stages of the garden can save you much weeding after planting.

As the garden matures, watch for those rock garden plants with rapid growth rates. Clip them back and dig out underground runners to control their spread.

Most rock garden plants will need regular watering during dry periods. A few, mostly those lower-elevation residents of the plains or desert, need to become quite dry between waterings in the summer.

Because the soil mix in the rock garden is so porous, nutrients will be leached from it quickly. Though a few rock garden plants tolerate very low fertility, a spring fertilization with a balanced garden fertilizer—or with pulverized, aged manure and bone meal—can be helpful.

Just as other perennials need division and replanting every few years, most rock garden plants (usually perennials) require this too. Work through the garden about every three years (or do part each year), lifting and dividing the spreading clumps. Replant them, or share them with your friends.

Penstemon rupicola thrives in a rock garden near Boston. It is planted between pieces of Tuffa rock, a porous, lightweight limestone-type rock which is ideal for rockeries.

Plants for rock gardens

Eastern Rock Garden

The plants recommended in these lists are for sunny rock gardens. Plants suitable for shady areas can be found in the forest lists.

Asclepias tuberosa	Butterflyweed	Showy orange flowers
Asclepias viridifolia	Green milkweed	Subtle but elegant; to 3 feet
Ceanothus americanus	New Jersey tea	Shrub; cluster of small white flowers
Dodecatheon meadia	Shooting-star	Emblem of American Rock Garden Society
Epigaea repens	Trailing arbutus	Shade; sandy or rocky acid soil
Gaultheria procumbens	Wintergreen	Under oaks or evergreens; sandy soils preferred
Gentiana andrewsii	Bottle gentian	Closed flowers
Gentiana autumnalis	Pine barren gentian	Showy; sandy soil
Gentiana crinita	Fringed gentian	Biennial
Gentiana puberulenta	Downy gentian	Very showy
Houstonia caerulea	Bluets	Dwarf floriferous clumps; pale purple flowers with gold centers
Hypoxis hirsuta	Yellow star grass	Miniature golden "lily"
Iris cristata	Dwarf crested iris	Purple flowers; light shade
Lilium philadelphicum	Prairie lily	Upright orange lilies
Lithospermum canescens	Puccoon	Showy golden "fiddleheads"
Lithospermum incisum	Fringed puccoon	Lemon-yellow flowers
Lupinus perennis	Wild lupine	Flowers blue and showy
Pedicularis canadensis	Wood betony	Flowers red or yellow
Phlox bifida	Cleft phlox	Pale blue to white, occasionally darker; very dwarf
Phlox pilosa	Downy phlox	Bright pink
Phlox subulata	Moss phlox	Including cultivars; floriferous
Polygala sanguinea	Field milkwort	Tight clusters of showy rose bracts
Rhexia virginica and *R. mariana*	Meadow beauty	Rose
Silene virginica	Fire pink	Bright red, star-shaped flowers
Tephrosia virginiana	Goat's rue	Showy, bicolored flowers in rose and yellow

Western Rock Garden

Aquilegia saximontana, A. flavescens, and *A. jonesii*	Columbine	Light shade; blue flowers
Arctostaphylos uva-ursi	Kinnikinick	Low shrub; excellent ground cover
Calochortus species	Mariposa lilies	Several types
Campanula piperi	Piper's bellflower	Tiny, with large purple star-shaped bellflowers
Dodecatheon alpinum and species *clevelandii, hendersonii,* and *poeticum*	Shooting-star	Cluster of basal leaves; hanging clusters of pink-to-rose flowers
Douglasia laevigata	Primrose family	Loosely tufted; rose-pink flowers
Dryas octopetala	Mountain avens	Basal rosettes of dark green leaves bear large white flowers
Eriogonum umbellatum	Sulphurflower	Silver basal leave rosettes; flowers bright yellow to cream
Erythronium species	Trout liles, avalanche lilies	All are good, but the higher elvation species are hard to grow
Fritillaria species	Fritillaries	Aside from *F. pudica* and *F. lanceolata,* most species are now very rare in the wild
Gentiana calycosa (also *algida, newberryi, oregana*)	Gentians	Showy white or deep purple bell-shaped flowers in fall
Geum triflorum	Prairie smoke	Red pendant flowers; fluffy seed heads resemble smoke
Heuchera sanguinea	Coral bells	Basal rosette of leaves; spikes of showy flowers
Heuchera cylindrica	White coral bells	White flowers
Iris douglasiana	Iris	Most are purple, some yellow-flowered
Kalmia poliifolia	American laurel	Moist, peaty soil; evergreen shrub to 2 feet with showy rose flowers
Lewisia cotyledon (also species *columbiana, leana, rediviva*)	Lewisias	All species require the perfect drainage of scree or a good gravel mulch
Lupinus nanus (many other dwarf species)	Lupine	Deep blue flowers
Penstemon davidsonii (also species *newberryi, pinifolius, rupicola*)	Penstemon	Most of these dwarf penstemons are shrubby, with rose or scarlet flowers
Phlox hoodii	Phlox	Gravel or sand mulch a must; cushion plant with silver foliage and white-to-rose flowers
Phlox nana	Phlox	Gravel or sand mulch a must; needlelike leaves and large deep pink flowers
Psilostrophe cooperi	Paper daisy	Dwarf clumps of yellow daisies which dry in place; used in dried arrangements
Pulsatilla patens	Pasqueflower	Showy purple crocuslike flowers in early spring
Salix anglorum antiplasta	Dwarf willow	Ground-hugging (trailing) form
Satureja douglasii	Oregon tea or Yerba Buena	Trailing evergreen with aromatic foliage; excellent ground cover
Silene acaulis	Moss campion	Cushion with small, bright pink flowers
Sisyrinchium douglasii	Blue-eyed grass	Purple-eyed grass; purple or lavender flowers;
Sisyrinchium bellum	Blue-eyed grass	Dark blue flowers; leaves like miniature iris
Townsendia exscapa and *T. hookeri*	Easter daisies	Clumps of silvery leaves, bearing white daisies with yellow centers
Viola hallii	Violet	Flowers dark violet and yellow or white
Zinnia grandiflora	Wild zinnia	Yellow flowers do not resemble garden zinnias

Southern Rock Gardens

Camassia hyacinthina	Wild hyacinth	Spring-blooming bulb; blue flowers
Clematis crispa	Dwarf clematis	Flowers showy and fragrant
Dicentra eximia	Bleeding-heart	Pink-to-purple flowers; semi-shade
Eustoma grandiflorum	Tulip gentian	Deep purple; showy
Gentiana andrewsii	Bottle gentian	Clusters of gentian blue "bottles" in autumn
Hypoxis hirsuta	Yellow stargrass	Tiny yellow "lilies"
Iris verna	Dwarf iris	Violet-blue to white
Liatris squarrosa	Scaly blazing-star	Spikes of large purple flowers
Lupinus texensis	Texas bluebonnets	State flower of Texas
Monarda didyma	Scarlet beebalm	Showy clusters of bright red flowers
Oxalis violacea	Violet wood sorrel	Dwarf; leaves like clover; flowers little lavender bells
Phlox divaricata	Wild sweet William	Blue; shade or semishade
Phlox pilosa species ozarkana	Prairie phlox	Southern subspecies; pink, sunloving
Phlox subulata	Phlox	Dwarf; red, pink, or white flowers; sun
Shortia galacifolia	Oconee bells	Shade; first-rate alpine plant
Silene virginica	Fire pink	Bright red flowers with five star-shaped notched petals
Sisyrinchium angustifolium	Blue-eyed grass	Blue flowers; forms large clumps
Viola pedata	Bird's foot violet	Southern forms available
Xyris iridifolia	Yellow-eyed grass	Wet sandy or peaty sites; yellow flowers
Yucca filamentosa and Y. gloriosa	Spanish daggers	Showy flower stalks to about 6 feet tall

For more information about plants for rock gardens

Eastern Rock Gardens

Rock Gardens, by Wilhelm Schacht. Universe Books, NY. 1981. Third Edition, edited by Jim Archibald.

A general book on rock gardening.

Rock Garden Plants, by Doretta Klaber. Henry Holt, NY. 1959.

A concise and valuable account by one of the United States' pioneer rock gardeners.

Western Rock Gardens

Western American Alpines, by Ira Gabrielson. Macmillan, NY. 1932.

Long out of print, but provides cultural instructions and encyclopedia of some of the best western North American wildflowers of good alpine form. Claude Barr's Jewels of the Plains *(see High Plains) was written as a companion volume to this classic.*

The Genus Lewisia, by R. C. Elliott. Alpine Garden Society Bulletin 34: 1-76. 1966 (also reprinted).

A wonderful little book. Elliott quotes extensively from the writings and correspondence of the great contemporary Lewisia explorers and growers, producing an archetypal botanical adventure story.

Rock Gardening, A Guide to Growing Alpines and Other Wildflowers in the American Garden, by H. Lincoln Foster. Bonanza Books, NY. 1968.

One of the classic texts on rock gardening. Contains a large encyclopedia of rock garden plants.

Southern Rock Gardens

Natives Preferred, by Caroline Dormon. Claitor's Publishing Division, Baton Rouge, LA. 1965.

Flowers Native to the Deep South, by Caroline Dormon. Claitor's Publishing Division, Baton Rouge, LA. 1958.

Both of Dormon's books cover landscaping with all groups of southern plants, including rock garden plants. Emphasis is on trees, shrubs, and herbs with showy flowers.

In a California beach garden, a dune shelters a planting of conifers. The boardwalk, bleached to the color of the sand, allows strollers to get a firm footing to appreciate such small treats as the bright red Indian paintbrush.

Seaside gardens

The seashore is a harsh environment for plants. Though the climate is free from extreme heat and cold, wind can be almost constant, soils are porous and nutrient-poor, and plants must tolerate salt spray and occasional inundation by salt water. Most plants adapted to the seashore have very large and intricate root systems. These not only mine the sandy soil for nutrients, but also help secure the plant in the wind and unstable soil.

The first rank of plants next to the beach usually consists of low, spreading plants that are very tolerant of saline soils and salt spray. Behind these come the dune grasses, stabilizing the sand, then forbs and shrubs growing among the grasses. Your seaside garden can use the native coastal plants of your region, imitating the natural landscape while bringing additional color, texture, and interest to the garden.

Design

Study natural seashore areas near you, and attractive seaside gardens. How does nature use plants to cover the sand, and gradually reclaim open areas? What native plants of your coastal area do you want to include in your garden? Note the pioneer small forbs and grasses that grow nearest to the beach and the species of trees and shrubs that grow on stabilized soils farther back from the water. Notice what does well in other gardens and what nurseries in the area have to offer. In all these settings, learn about the natives of your coastal region—these will be the easiest plants to establish in your garden.

It is difficult to build a seaside garden quickly. It requires several years of gradually reclaiming open sand or poor soil, getting the pioneer forbs and grasses established, then gradually adding shrubs and trees. This process establishes more favorable microclimates for plant growth, and makes each successive planting possible. In planting a seaside garden, you are speeding up the process of natural succession in your area.

Because most seaside gardens are made in sand, you will need to improve the soil for the plants to grow well. Add organic materials to large areas of the garden if you are planning large, organized beds, or planting species not quite adapted to

A sturdy board fence protects a coastal wooded area from blowing sand. The stately Monterey cypress in the foreground is sculpted by the wind. It's one of the few trees that do well near windswept beaches.

the seashore. If you are imitating the open, scattered natural plantings of the seashore, amend the soil more simply by adding organic materials such as nitrified sawdust or compost to each planting hole.

Wind may be a factor in your design. Early in the design process, decide where you need windbreaks and which views you want to leave open, then work out a compromise plan for the windbreaks. If you need a windbreak in some areas where trees would block the view, use low shrubs or a stone wall instead.

Your main planting goals are twofold: first, of course, you want to create an attractive garden. Secondly, but no less important, you need to stabilize the sand and grainy soils with your plants. With this in mind, try to cover almost every square foot of your garden soil with some grass, forb, trailing vine, shrub, or tree.

To prevent erosion of the soil and destruction of the shallow surface roots of the plants, design raised walks through your seaside garden. Boardwalks are very attractive, or you can use paths of gravel, flat paving stones, or wood chips.

Further back from the shore, you may want to grow other types of native plants. Depending on your region, the most natural neighbors to seashore grasses and shrubs may be bog plants, a dense shrubland or chaparral, or a forest garden.

Planting

Starting with plants rather than seeds will help establish a seaside garden most quickly. Seeding will not be as

easy, because of the dry soil and harsh conditions. Get the plants you want at local coastal nurseries, or from state conservation agencies in some areas. Don't try to transplant beach plants from the wild; because of their huge root systems, it is a difficult process. If you cannot find the plants you want from a commercial source, you may want to try raising them from collected seed or from cuttings.

If you are planning to grow some species from seed, it will probably be easy to find plenty of seed in the wild. The trick is to get it germinated and grown into seedlings without having it dry out in the sun and wind. If you are sowing the seed directly into the garden area, prepare the area with some organic soil amendment and use ample amounts of seed to allow for poor germination. For surer results, sow the seed in flats or pots of good soil, and plant them out after one or two seasons' growth.

Seedlings should be planted with a rootball of good soil for their nutrition and stability. Plants without a good rootball can easily be blown over in a strong wind. In difficult spots, set the plant into the ground within a porous container such as a wire basket filled with good soil. The addition of a time-released fertilizer will help to establish the plants.

All your plants will need frequent watering until they are established, because sandy soils dry out quickly.

Maintenance

Most plants growing in sandy soils need fertilization at least once a year, in spring. Use a balanced lawn and garden fertilizer, and give a second application in early summer to plants that are still growing vigorously then. The hardiest grass and shrub beach dwellers will not need this fertilization after a few years, but it will help them get started.

Another way to provide plant nutrients and to improve soil is by mulching. Any organic material makes a useful mulch, including seaweed (preferably with the salt washed off). Coarser, fibrous materials will last longer and stay put better in the wind.

Regular watering will be needed the first several seasons, several times a week right after planting, decreasing to a few deep waterings during each growing season. After several years, the toughest seashore natives can do without extra watering.

Coccoloba uvifera (sea grape) *is a subtropical coastal native.*

Plants for seaside gardens
Atlantic and Gulf Coasts

Trees

Ilex opaca	American holly	Holiday wreath holly
Juniperus virginiana	Eastern red cedar	Widespread evergreen
Pinus rigida	Pitch pine	Can be mixed with oaks
Pinus taeda	Loblolly pine	Fast-growing
Pinus virginiana	Virginia pine	Short-lived; shade intolerant
Pithecolobium flexicaule	Texas ebony	Northernmost tropical mimosa
Prunus maritima	Beach plum	Straggling; to 10 feet
Quercus marilandica	Blackjack oak	Scrub oak species
Quercus shumardii	Shumard oak	Large southern red oak
Quercus stellata	Post oak	Scrub oak or small tree
Quercus virginiana	Live oak	Deep South only

Shrubs

Erythrina herbacea	Coralbean	Sandy soil; tolerates salt spray; scarlet poisonous seeds
Hibiscus palustris	Swamp rose-mallow	5 to 6 feet; flowers like hollyhocks
Ilex decidua	Possum haw	Deciduous holly with orange or red fruits
Ilex glabra	Inkberry	Black fruit; multiple stems
Ipomoea pes-caprae	Railroad vine	Native to West Indies; purple-to-red morning glory flowers
Leucophyllum frutescens	Texas silverleaf	Sandy soils; gray leaves with pink-lavender flowers
Myrica cerifera	Southern wax myrtle	Tolerant of salt spray
Sapindus drummondii	Chinaberry	Black berries; contains the poison *saponin*
Yucca aloifolia, filamentosa, and *gloriosa*	Spanish bayonet	White or violet flowers

Grasses

Ammophila breviligulata	Marram grass	Stabilizes drifting dune sands
Andropogon virginicus	Broomsedge	Dominant in coastal marshes
Andropogon littoralis	Bluestem	Solid, coarse stems
Panicum species	Switchgrass	Inquire locally for correct species
Spartina spartinae	Cordgrass	Dominant in coastal marshes
Uniola latifolia	Spike grass	Straw or violet-tinged flowers

Forbs

Arnica acaulis	Leopard's bane	Small sunflower
Gaillardia pulchella	Blanketflower	"Sunburst" pattern sunflower
Rhexia mariana	Maryland meadow beauty	Pink flowers
Solidago filstulosa	Pine barrens goldenrod	Yellow flowers
Solidago sempervirens	Seaside goldenrod	Plumelike flower heads

Western Seaside Gardens

Trees

Abies bracteata	Santa Lucia fir	Widely grown but native only to Santa Lucia Mountains of California
Abies grandis	Giant fir	To 300 feet; pendulous branches; flexible needles
Acer macrophyllum	Big-leaf maple	Large leaves turn to bright orange in fall; to 100 feet
Alnus rhombifolia	White alder	30–40 feet; gray bark; usually along streams
Arbutus menziesii	Madrone	80–120 feet; dark red bark peels to light orange inside; evergreen
Lithocarpus densiflorus	Tan oak	Link between oaks and chestnuts; abundant in coastal fog belt
Picea sitchensis	Sitka spruce	Pyramidal tree to 200 feet, with great arching, drooping branches
Pinus contorta	Shore pine	Grows on sandy soils and rarely reaches 30 feet
Pinus contorta var. *latifolia*	Lodgepole pine	Tall tree of the Sierras, Cascades, and Rockies
Pinus radiata	Monterey pine	Widely planted; 80–100 feet with cones that open only after fires
Pinus muricata	Bishop pine	To 40–50 feet
Pinus remorata	Santa Cruz Island pine	To 50–60 feet
Pseudotsuga menziesii	Douglas fir	To 200 feet; bluish foliage
Sequoia sempervirens	Redwood	Grows with Douglas fir, tan oak, and California bay in narrow coastal strip of Oregon and California; to 340 feet
Umbellularia californica	California bay	75–100 feet; aromatic evergreen leaves can be substituted for bay leaves in cooking

Shrubs

Arctostaphylos	Manzanita	Many coastal species; evergreen; white to pink flowers
Ceanothus species	Redroot	Deciduous or evergreen shrubs or trees
Coreopsis gigantea	Sea dahlia	Stem succulent; ferny, deciduous foliage; clusters of yellow daisies
Garrya elliptica	Silk-tassel bush	To 25 feet; late winter, early spring blooms
Lupinus arboreus	Bush lupine	To 6–8 feet; sulphur-yellow flowers
Myrica californica	California wax myrtle	To 35 feet; evergreen
Rhododendron macrophyllum	California rosebay	Corolla rose to rose-purple and spotted brown
Rhododendron occidentale	Western azalea	Fragrant flowers, pink-tinged with white corolla

Forbs

Brodiaea laxa	Ithuriel's spear	Spherical clusters of light blue to dark purple flowers
Calochortus luteus	Yellow Mariposa lily	Erect, deep yellow flowers
Clarkia amoena	Farewell-to-spring	Light pink flowers with deep red centers
Clarkia rubicunda	Farewell-to-spring	South of the Golden Gate; light pink flowers
Delphinium nudicaule (*D. cardinale* south of Monterey County)		
	Scarlet larkspur	Very showy
Erysimum concinnum and *E. franciscanum*	Wallflowers	Very fragrant clusters of cream-to-yellow flowers
Iris douglasiana and *I. longipetala*	Iris	Pale blue to deep purple flowers; coastal species
Koeleria cristata	Junegrass	To 2 feet in California; straw color; dormant by late summer
Linanthus grandiflorus	Linanthus	Annual; clusters of 1-inch, white, funnelform flowers
Lupinus densiflorus	Lupine	Annual; to 2½ feet with white, blue, rose, violet, yellow, or orange flowers
Lupinus nanus	Lupine	Annual, to 1½ feet, with deep blue flowers
Paeonia californica	Wild peony	Similar to garden peony, but much smaller; red-brown petals
Stipa pulchra	Needlegrass	Clump grass with drooping clusters of long-awned seeds, from which its name comes
Wyethia angustifolia and *W. glabra*	Mule-ears	Clusters of strap-shaped basal leaves; large sunflowers on 12- to 18-inch stems
Zauschneria californica	California fuchsia	Small shrub of sunny, rocky slopes; tubular red flowers attract hummingbirds

For more information about plants for seaside gardens

Western seaside gardens

See also chaparral gardens.

Wild Flowers of California, by Mary Elizabeth Parsons. Dover Publications Inc., NY. 1966.

Hardy Californians, by Lester Rowntree. Peregrine Smith, Inc., Salt Lake City, UT. 1980.

These two classics give almost poetical descriptions and accounts of how to grow some of the most popular California wildflowers. Both volumes are generously illustrated.

Northeastern seaside gardens

Gardening by the Sea, Daniel Foley. Chilton Book Co., Radnor, PA. 1974.

Southeastern seaside gardens

Coastal Plants of Florida, by Lacey F. Bullard. Florida Division of Forestry, Tallahassee, FL.

Growing Natives, Richard W. Workman. Sanibel-Cappiva Conservation Foundation Inc., Sanibel, FL. 1980.

Bluff wallflower is one of several mustard relatives that has adapted to conditions near the beach.

A native cypress swamp was used as the basis for this swamp garden at Magnolia Gardens in South Carolina. Exotics, such as the Chinese wisteria climbing the tree, add color and are in keeping with the habitat.

Subtropical gardens

The only true subtropical region in the continental United States lies in the southern part of Florida, but subtropical gardens can be planted in any frost-free area with warm summers. This includes many areas on the Gulf coast, and the California coast south of Santa Barbara.

If you live very near or on the coast, use salt-tolerant species. Coastal environments also have brilliant sun, glare, wind, surface drought, and heat. Choose adapted native species. It is difficult to coax others to do well in this harsh environment.

Interest in gardening with the native plants of southern Florida is strong and growing. The Florida Native Plant Society has active chapters in many counties and these can provide you with suggestions of native plants to use and ideas for your landscape design.

This interest is motivated by several factors. First, many native Florida species are disappearing as their native wetland, forest, and beach habitats are being destroyed for development. Bringing the native plants of this region into the garden is an important way of preserving many species. Another reason is that subtropical plants are the best suited to the region, and will be the easiest to grow in difficult soils and with minimal supplemental watering. Water for landscape irrigation is becoming scarce in many parts of south Florida, and may be rationed in future periods of drought. The soils of this region are highly variable, and may be shallow and very acidic, alkaline, or have a layer of acidic leaf litter atop an alkaline subsoil. Plants native to each type of soil and geographic area will tolerate these conditions easily, and will grow well with little care once they are established in the garden.

Design

Begin your design with a thorough site analysis. The texture, depth, and pH of your soils can be critical to plant growth. County extension agents can test your soil and advise you on plants that are adapted to it. Study the microclimates of your site. What areas get hot in summer? Shade trees can help cool these spots and can be especially important on the east, west, and south sides of your house. If you want the sun to warm your house in winter, plant winter-deciduous trees on the south side.

What about soil water? You may have areas that remain wet all year or become saturated only during the rainy season. You may also have extremely dry areas of porous, sandy soil where you may wonder if anything will grow. Match these site habitats to similar plant communities near you, and try to design the garden using plants from these communities. That dry, sandy area may be ideal for some of the trees and shrubs of the sand pine scrub communities. A wetland can become a focal point for the garden and, properly planted, can provide shelter for birds and other wildlife. Beach and dune natives will help stabilize soils in coastal areas and can tolerate saline soils there.

In all of this, you can be helped by two sources: your local county extension agent and the nearest chapter of the Florida Native Plant Society. Both may have lists of well-adapted native plants for your area.

Design your landscape so it needs no supplemental watering during the dry season. Water conservation is becoming very important in many parts of south Florida, and there are native species that can tolerate several months of drought each year during the dry season. Of course, even drought-tolerant plants need extra watering during the first year or two.

Use the topography of your site to assist you with water conservation. Plant the most drought-tolerant shrubs and trees on high ground and porous soils, and place those that require more water in the swales and heavier soils, where ground water is available during more of the year.

Before finishing your plan be sure the plants you have selected are available. Many more native species are becoming available each year from commercial sources, but some availability problems still occur.

Planting

Choosing plants that will tolerate

your soils means you don't have to do large-scale soil amendment, except in garden areas intended for special plants such as rhododendrons, roses, or other exotic species.

Dig large holes (up to 16 inches in diameter for a standard 1-gallon can), and then refill most of the hole with native soil. This opens up an area for the roots, and will encourage them to grow into the area beyond the planting hole. A chemical "wetting agent" may be useful, as will time-released fertilizer. Spread a deep mulch, even around ground cover plants.

Begin your planting with the trees, so they can become established rapidly. Then add the shrubs and ground covers as your budget and time allow. When planting a hardwood hammock, you need not wait until all the trees are in and growing to plant the understory trees and shrubs; most of these species are sun-tolerant.

The new plants will need extra watering during their first one or two seasons, but will eventually be drought-tolerant. An organic mulch spread around each plant will help conserve the needed water.

Plants for subtropical gardens

Trees

Acacia farnesiana	Sweet acacia	Fluffly, yellow flower heads
Annona glabra	Pond apple	Fruits egg-shaped, to 6 inches long
Bursera simaruba	West Indian birch	Copper-red bark peels in attractive patterns
Coccoloba uvifera	Sea grape	Clusters of edible, grapelike fruit; large leaves
Conocarpus erectus	Green buttonwood	Also var. *sericeus* (silver buttonwood); shrub to small tree
Cordia sebestena	Geiger tree	Orange flowers; white, egglike fruits
Ficus aurea	Strangler fig	Evergreen; sometimes starts as epiphyte on trees such as cabbage palm, eventually killing them
Ficus citrifolia	Shortleaf fig	Good shade tree; to 60 feet
Lysiloma latisiligua	Wild tamarind	Feathery foliage
Mastichodendron foetidissimum	Mastic tree	Coastal shade tree of southern Florida; slow-growing
Pinus elliottii	Slash pine	To 100 feet; yields timber, resin, and turpentine
Piscidia piscipula	Jamaica dogwood	Fast-growing flowering shade tree
Quercus virginiana	Live oak	Evergreen; to 60 feet
Roystonea elata	Royal palm	To 80 feet; considered most handsome native palm
Sabal palmetto	Cabbage palm	Florida's state tree; to 90 feet
Simarouba glauca	Paradise tree	Yellow flowers; undersides of leaves silvery
Swietenia mahagoni	Mahogany	Valuable tropical timber tree; very rare because of logging; to 50 feet
Zanthoxylum fagara	Wild lime	To 20 feet; spiny branches; used as hedge

Shrubs

Chrysobalanus var. *icaco*	Coco palm	To 12 feet; edible, plumlike fruit
Erythrina herbacea	Coral bean	Bright red flowers and bright red, poisonous seeds
Hamelia patens	Firebush	To 25 feet; scarlet or orange flowers
Myrica cerifera	Wax myrtle	Evergreen leaves; gray-white fruit
Psychotria undata	Wild coffee	Red berries attract birds; also species *ligustrifolia, nervosa,* and *sulzneri*
Randia aculeata	White indigo berry	White berries
Serenoa repens	Saw palmetto	Green or blues leaves; prostrate or creeping
Sophora tomentosa	Necklace pod	Wisterialike flower clusters; seeds of some species poisonous
Zamia floridana	Coontie	Short trunk, sometimes underground

Wildflowers and Grasses

Asclepias tuberosa	Butterfly weed	To 3 feet; orange corolla
Borrichia arborescens	Sea oxeye	Rayless yellow daisies on gray-green mats; ground cover; salt-tolerant (*B. frutescens* is more compact)
Canavalia maritima	Bay bean	Viny plant of beaches and dunes; ground cover and erosion control on sand; showy pink to purple flowers
Conocarpus	Silver buttonwood	Shrubs or trees of mangrove swamps
Coreopsis leavensorthii	Tickseed	
Ernodea littoralis	Golden creeper	Protected
Gaillardia pulchella	Firewheel	Disc yellow flowers or with red tips
Guapira discolor	Blolly	
Hamelia patens	Firebush	To 25 feet; scarlet or orange flowers
Helianthus debilis	Beach sunflower	Disc flowers deep red-purple
Hymenocallis latifolia	Spider lily	Spectacular white flowers on amaryllislike plants; to 3 feet
Ipomoea pes-caprae	Railroad vine	Creeping; to 60 feet
Lantana depressa	Pineland lantana	
Liatris spicata	Blazing-star	To 5 feet; purple bracts
Portulaca pilosa	Moss rose	Small red flowers, ½ inch or less across
Rhexia species	Meadow beauty	Moist locations; to 2 feet
Rudbeckia hirta	Brown-eyed Susan	Disk flowers brown-purple; to 3 feet
Sisyrinchium species	Blue-eyed grass	Grasslike linear leaves; clump-forming
Uniola paniculata	Sea oats	Abundant beach grass from Virginia to Gulf of Mexico
Verbena maritima	Beach verbena	Lavender flowers; salt tolerant; ground cover
Yucca aloifolia	Spanish-bayonet	White flowers tinged with purple; to 25 feet

Wisteria frutescens *is a native wisteria hardy to zone 5.*

For more information about plants for subtropical gardens

Plants for the South, A Guide for Landscape Design, by Neil G. Odenwald and James R. Turner. Claitor's Publishing Division, Baton Rouge, LA. 1980.

Extensive encyclopedia of horticulturally valuable plants of the South.

A Flora of Tropical Florida: A Manual of the Seed Plants and Ferns of Southern Peninsular Florida, by Robert W. and Olga Lakela. University of Miami Press, Coral Gables, FL. 1976.

Growing Native: Native Plants for Landscape Use in Coastal South Florida, by Richard W. Workman. Sanibel-Captiva Conservation Foundations, Inc., Sanibel, FL. 1980.

If your garden borders on water, or is on poorly drained land, choose trees that prefer wet soil, like sweet gum (Liquidamber styraciflua).

Water gardens

If you have a natural stream, pond, or even a wet spot in your garden, you can develop it into a centerpiece for your native landscape. Water and plants go together beautifully in any garden; in yours, the water can provide special habitats for native stream, pool, and bog plants.

Where to plant a water garden

A flat, wet area is a difficult planting spot for many gardens. Since none of the dry-land plants you try there will grow well, why not create an environment for wetland species? Begin by varying the contours of the area. Dig out the wettest spot by hand, or rent a backhoe to make the job easier. The central basin will now collect and hold water, and may naturally become a shallow pond with excavation. Pile the soil up around the pool to create higher ground. By these simple measures you have formed three habitats for wetland plants: a pool for those that grow in standing water, bog areas for plants preferring constantly wet soil, and areas of moist soil on the high ground where you can grow typical streamside forbs, shrubs, and trees.

A drainage ditch crossing your property creates another opportunity for growing wetland plants. First be sure that the ditch doesn't carry pollutants, then widen it in one or more areas to create bog conditions.

A natural stream is a boon to any garden. In many cases, you won't have to do anything to the stream but set in plants along the banks, but you may want to make small changes in its course by reshaping its banks or widening some areas to create pools. You may even dam the stream to create a pool. Before doing this, check with your neighbors along the stream and with your local government (it may be illegal to alter a natural stream flow in your community).

You can create other garden water elements by piping in water to the garden, creating a pool, cascade, or more formal water feature where none existed before. We haven't room here to discuss the plumbing and construction methods for establishing this kind of pool, but a number of gardening books give instructions.

Planting

Design your water garden according to the soil and water preferences of each plant species. Some water plants are true aquatics, growing submerged in water. Others grow in saturated soil that is occasionally flooded. Still others grow in moist soil, and do not easily tolerate flooding.

Soils in a wetland are usually classified as peat (undecomposed organic material), muck (decomposed organic material), or mineral (mostly sand, silt, and clay). Each water plant does best in one of these types of soil, with a paticular amount of available moisture. Arrange those with similar needs together.

Plant limited numbers of aggressive aquatic species, especially in a small garden; such plants can easily take over. Some water plants do get quite large. Choose smaller species for small pools.

Most water plants can be easily propagated by division in the spring. Planting techniques in the water garden vary according to the depth of water. On moist ground, broadcast dry seeds onto the prepared soil or set plants into enriched pockets of soil. In areas with standing water, you can use several planting techniques. In shallow water, set plants into the mud just beneath the water level and place stones over the rootballs to keep them from floating upward. Or place the plants in containers with a good garden soil (don't use soilless potting mixes), water the soil well and cover with gravel, and set the containers into the bottom soil of the pond. This method also can be used in deep water. Or you can wrap the rootballs of small plants or bundles of several cuttings in balls of clay and drop them onto the soft bottom of the pool.

Paths

Your water garden should be accessible from other parts of the garden, for viewing and strolling. Boardwalks make attractive paths. The wood should be treated with a copper-based wood preservative, because other types of wood preservative can poison fish and plants. Another type of path can be made from large stone slabs laid across shallow water areas.

Maintenance

Weeding is as important here as in any garden. Be sure before starting the garden that no difficult perennial aquatic weeds, such as quackgrass or reed canary grass, are present; eradicate them if they are.

Algae are a type of weed unique to water gardens. There are two types of algae: one is a hairlike growth on the sides of the pond. This type helps to keep the water clear. A few snails grazing on this algae will help prevent excessive growth.

A fast-moving stream or a small waterfall adds soothing water music to your garden as a more formal fountain would do. Natives like this yellow-flowered Caltha palustris *can cling to water-washed stream banks.*

The second type of algae is unicellular. This algae makes pond water look like pea soup. Although it can be temporarily controlled with an algicide, the algae will return as soon as the algicide is gone from the water. The key to keeping the pond water clear is in establishing a balance of plants and animals in the pond. The higher plants are your most valuable aids in controlling algae. They compete for light, dissolved carbon dioxide, and nutrients in the water. Grasses are most effective in preventing algae. Waterlilies are also helpful because they shade the water.

Animals help in two ways. Some of them, such as snails, tadpoles, and fresh-water clams, eat the algae. Also, snails and tadpoles are scavengers, cleaning up the leftover fish food and droppings. Fish will only eat fresh food. At each feeding, only give them what they will eat up in five minutes.

Filters are also effective in keeping pond water clear. They remove the algae, and also leftover fish food and other particles in the water. If you have a pump already planned for your water garden, plan to install a filter in the system. Clean filters periodically according to the manufacturer's directions.

When you fill a pool or pond, even if you have just emptied it to clean it, it will become cloudy for a while. It usually takes from one to three months for it to clear again as the natural balance is restored. If you wish, you can keep it clear during this period with an algicide. The water might also cloud up as a response to seasonal changes.

Mosquitos can be controlled by small fish, such as mosquito fish (*Gambusia*), which are native to North America. Goldfish are also excellent for eating mosquito larvae.

Pointederia cordata *is a true aquatic, rooting at the bottom of the pond. Plant it by burying a container in your pond or by weighting the roots so they won't float before they are established.*

Plants for water gardens
Streamside and Pond-Edge plants
(Tolerant of continually moist soil and occasional flooding.)

Trees

Acer grandidentatum	Bigtooth maple	Rockies and Southwest
Acer macrophyllum	Big-leaf maple	Pacific coast; to 100 feet
Alnus species	Alders	About 30 species (vary across U.S.); moist soils, cool climates
Fraxinus pennsylvanica	Green ash	Atlantic through the Rockies; to 60 feet
Larix laricina	Tamarack	Deciduous conifer of the Northeast
Liquidambar styraciflua	Sweet gum	Eastern U.S., fall color
Magnolia virginiana	Sweet bay magnolia	Eastern U.S.; semievergreen; large fragrant flowers
Nyssa sylvatica	Sour gum	Eastern U.S.; fall color; to 100 feet
Picea glauca	White spruce	Northeast; blue-green leaves
Picea pungens	Colorado blue spruce	Rockies and Pacific Northwest; to 100 feet
Platanus species	Sycamores	*P. occidentalis* in East; *P. racemosa* in California; *P. wrightii* in Arizona and New Mexico
Populus species	Poplars	30–40 species (vary across U.S.); easy to cultivate
Salix species	Mountain ash	Clusters of bright orange berries; *S. americana* in East; *S. sitchensis* and *S. occidentalis* in the West
Umbellularia californica	California bay	Pacific Coast; large tree with aromatic foliage

Shrubs

Calycanthus floridus	Carolina allspice	Southern U.S.; to 10 feet
Calycanthus occidentalis	Spice bush	In California; flowers reddish
Cephalanthus occidentalis	Buttonbush	Eastern U.S.; to 20 feet
Clematis species	Clematis	Showy vines; *C. pitcheri* in the East; *C. pseudoalpina* and many others in West
Clethra alnifolia	Sweet pepperbush	Eastern U.S.; very fragrant white to pink flowers; forms clumps
Cornus stolonifera	Red osier dogwood	Transcontinental; easy cultivation
Ilex glabra	Inkberry	Eastern U.S.; evergreen holly with black fruits
Myrica species	Wax myrtles	Eastern and Pacific Coast evergreen shrubs
Prunus virginiana	Western choke cherry	Fruit used in jellies
Viburnum lentago	Nannyberry	Black berries; forms thickets
Viburnum trilobum	Highbush cranberry	Bright red berries

Forbs

Asclepias incarnata	Swamp milkweed	Showy pink flowers
Eupatorium maculatum	Joe-pye weed	Showy purple flowers
Helenium autumnale	Sneezeweed	Yellow flowers; to 5 feet
Lilium species	Lilies	*L. michiganese*, many others in East; *L. pardalinum*, many others in West
Lobelia cardinalis	Cardinal flower	Transcontinental; scarlet flowers
Lobelia siphilitica	Great blue lobelia	Eastern U.S.; to 3 feet
Lysichiton americanum	Western skunk cabbage	Leaves to 5 feet long
Mimulus species	Monkeyflower	Primarily in western U.S.; most species are showy
Monarda didyma	Scarlet beebalm	Eastern U.S.; very showy
Symplocarpus foetidus	Skunk cabbage	Strangely beautiful; purple and green foliage; eastern U.S.

Semiaquatics
(Grow near water, or with their "feet" occasionally in shallow water.)

Angelica atropurpurea (other species in West)	Angelica	Large spherical umbels; tall and stately
Acorus calamus	Sweet flag	Transcontinental; aromatic; to 6 feet
Asclepias incarnata	Swamp milkweed	Pink showy flowers
Betula lutea	Yellow birch	Eastern species; brown peeling bark
Calamagrostis canadensis	Bluejoint grass	To 6 feet; pink inflorescences
Caltha palustris (*C. howellii* in California and Oregon)	Marsh marigold	Flowers like giant golden buttercups
Cephalanthus occidentalis	Buttonbush	Handsome shrub; transcontinental
Chelone glabra	Turtlehead	White flowers; host plant for Baltimore butterfly
Iris versicolor	Wild blue flag	Eastern U.S.; stems to 3 feet
Lobelia cardinalis	Cardinal flower	Brilliant scarlet flowers; transcontinental
Lobelia siphilitica	Great blue lobelia	Eastern U.S.; to 3 feet
Phragmites communis	Wild reed	To 8 feet; transcontinental
Physostegia virginiana	False dragonhead	Pink flowers; eastern U.S.
Quercus palustris	Pin oak	Eastern U.S.; widely planted for shade
Taxodium distichum	Bald cypress	Eastern U.S.; can also grow submerged in water
Typha species	Cattail	Transcontinental; about 15 species

True Aquatics
(Grow in water.)

Nelumbo lutea	American lotus	Giant peltate leaves; seed pods used in dried arrangements
Nuphar species	Yellow pond lilies	"Waterlilies;" transcontinental
Nymphaea tuberosa	Tuberous white waterlily	Flowers showy; tubers and seeds are prime duck foods
Peltandra virginica	Arrow arum	Also called "duck corn," referring to the greenish black fruits at base of the spadix
Pontederia cordata	Pickerel weed	Very handsome arrow-shaped leaves and purple flowers
Sagittaria species	Arrowhead	Arrow-shaped leaves; prime duck food
Sparganium eurycarpum	Giant bur weed	Spherical fruits bear corn-sized seeds which is food for waterfowl
Zizania aquatica	Wild rice	Requires current in the water

For more information about plants for water gardens

The Water Garden, by Frances Perry. Van Nostrand Reinhold, 1981.

Primarily a plant book, but also contains a discussion of pool construction.

Native plants in the city

The various parts of this book are written as much for the urban gardener as for those in the suburbs or rural areas. Native plants are the original vegetation of every part of the country, and many can adapt as well to city conditions as the exotic plants more typically found there.

City gardens are often smaller than their suburban or rural counterparts, but this need not deter you from using native plants. It may be difficult to develop a prairie or forest around a townhouse, but a small patio tree, shrub screen, or ground cover can be chosen from among the native plants of your region. In addition, smaller native wildflowers and flowering shrubs blend happily in flower beds with snapdragons and peonies, and a native plant rock garden can be very attractive in a sunny area.

How do you find natural landscapes to study if you live in the city? Try the same sources you would if you lived in the country: your state native plant society or wildflower preservation society, a local branch of the Nature Conservancy, or other conservation organizations. Also visit state parks, wildlife preserves, and national parks in your region.

Once you've done this, you will have to adapt what you've learned about your regional native plants and their habitats to your urban site. First analyze the plant habitats of your site—the microclimates, available water, and soils. In the city, you'll find the habitats very different from those in nearby natural areas: urban temperatures are usually higher; reflected heat and low humidity further increase the stress on plants; and soils are poor, stripped of topsoil, and may contain construction rubble or chemical contaminants. Air pollution may be significant in many areas.

All of these conditions will make life more difficult for your regional native plants than in their native forests or fields. In choosing those to plant, your best choices will be those that grow on difficult sites, in dry and stony or wet and poorly drained soil—those plants, in short, that seem to be able to grow anywhere. Trying to bring delicate, demanding native plants into the city may only be frustrating. Many plants native to coastal plains, prairies, desert, and chaparral environments are very hardy and tolerant, and can survive and grow in the city with proper care. The native plants of forested environments are sometimes more demanding of proper soil, humidity, and other conditions, but can be grown in city gardens.

When you can't find a native plant to fill a particular niche in your garden, look at the hardy exotic trees, shrubs, and ground covers in your area. A good source of information on native and exotic plants well adapted to city life in your region is the local agricultural extension service.

If you have a sizeable yard, it will be easy to find plants adapted to its habitats. If your lot is small or nonexistent (as for apartment dwellers), you may nonetheless want to grow

Natives form the backbone of this condominium garden in downtown Philadelphia — Magnolia virginiana *and* Cornus florida *(on left),* Ilex verticillata *(on right),* Parthenocissus quinquifolia *(climbing the wall in back).* **Exotic annuals add seasonal color.**

native plants in the city, and there are a number of ways to do this.

One way is to garden in containers on a balcony or windowsill. A grouping of native plants in containers can be arranged to suggest a natural setting outdoors. Larger containers, such as trough gardens, can be planted with several native plants to create a tiny, contained landscape. The Chinese and Japanese art of *bonkei* imitates a natural scene in a flat tray.

Another way is to seek out an urban gardening organization. Here you can band together with neighbors to beautify small and large areas in the city, growing food and ornamental gardens and planting the native trees and shrubs of your region.

On your own, you can get permission to plant a vacant lot or open area adjacent to your own property. Begin with trees to establish a better microclimate, and add shrubs, along with mixes of hardy annual and perennial wildflowers. Gardens like these can bring great beauty into the city.

Notes on lawns
A lawn is an attractive addition to the landscape. It is cool in the summer, trim-looking, and, by dint of regular fertilization, beautifully green. It provides an open space in a landscape otherwise crowded with flowers, shrubs, and trees, and is a fine playing surface for all kinds of games.

In order to maintain this beauty, the lawn requires regular water, large amounts of fertilizer, and a lot of weeding, mowing, and raking.

With this in mind, consider the alternatives. If the lawn is intended mainly as a visual element in the garden and will get little traffic, you can substitute a low-growing herbaceous or shrubby ground cover (many are identified in the plant lists in this chapter). If the area is to have traffic or occasional use as a play surface, substitute a hardier grass for the typical bluegrass or St. Augustine-grass lawn. In the Plains and Southwest, the native buffalo grass *(Buchloe dactyloides)* makes an attractive, gray-green turf that requires only occasional mowing, and less water than a conventional lawn. However, it is not as soft to sit or play on as conventional turfgrasses. In other parts of the country, tall fescue grass *(Festuca arundinacea)*, though not a native, can be mowed high and watered infrequently during most of the season.

For games, alternative play surfaces (depending on the type of games) are sawdust, bark chips, or other soft organic mulches that will pack down with traffic. Also stop to consider why only a flat, even surface will do as a play area: children more often prefer uneven ground, with the excitement of shrubs to hide behind and trees to climb. One Wisconsin advocate of native plant gardening suggests that if you eliminate the lawn, the children simply find other games to play in the new garden.

If you want a conventional grass lawn for a play area, or cannot resist its green appeal as a landscape element, here are some suggestions for minimizing its maintenance. First, plan the landscape so that only plants tolerant of regular watering are near the lawn, and channel the drainage from the lawn to avoid plantings that prefer drier soil. Prepare the soil deeply and well, with plenty of organic matter incorporated into the top few inches for sustained lawn health. Manage water carefully to encourage deep rooting of the grasses. Do this by watering infrequently and deeply once the lawn is established.

Other sources of information

This is a small book, so there isn't room to cover the native plants and horticultural methods of each region in detail. For readers who would like to explore the ecology of their region in more detail, here are some additional sources of information.

Books

For additional general information on plant ecology, the plant communities of North America, and plant propagation practices, see these books:

The Ecology of North America, by Victor E. Shelford. University of Illinois Press, Urbana, IL. 1978 (paperback).

Well-illustrated descriptions of major plants and animals of all North American communities from Panama to the Arctic.

Angiosperm Biogeography and Past Continental Movements, by Peter H. Raven and Daniel I. Axelrod. Missouri Botanical Garden, St. Louis, MO. 1981 (reprinted from a 1974 issue of the ***Annals of the Missouri Botanical Garden).***

The geological history of the flowering plants of the world, including theoretical speculation on the origin of the flowering plants in terms of the geological theory of continental drift.

Biology of Plants, Third Edition, by Peter H. Raven, Ray F. Evert, and Helena Curtis. Worth Publishers, Inc., New York. 1981.

This generously illustrated current textbook in introductory college botany is a valuable reference tool to add to your library.

Flowering Plants of the World, by V. H. Heywood. Mayflower Books, New York. 1978.

Gives descriptions, color illustrations, economic uses, and distribution maps for all the families of flowering plants. One of the most beautiful books on plants.

Terrestrial Plant Ecology, by Michael G. Barbour, Jack H. Burk, and Wanna D. Pitts. The Benjamin/Cummings Publishing Co., Inc., Menlo Park, CA. 1980.

This plant ecology textbook has a wealth of information on North American plants.

Directory to Resources on Wildflower Propagation, by Gene A. Sullivan and Richard H. Daley. National Council of State Garden Clubs, Inc., St. Louis, MO. 1981.

A directory of people and organizations involved in growing native plants.

Plant societies

One of the best sources of information on native plants is your state native plant society or wildflower preservation society. If your state does not have such a society, chances are that a neighboring state in your region does. Native plant societies offer information on native plant communities, propagation, and uses of native plants in gardens, along with many tours, lectures, and meetings.

Alabama Wildflower Society
c/o A. Leon Bates
246 James Place
Florence, AL 35630

Arizona Native Plant Society
c/o Dr. William McGinnies
530 E. Cambridge Drive
Tucson, AZ 85704

Arkansas Native Plant Society
c/o Don Peach
Route 1, Box 282
Mena, AR 71953

California Native Plant Society
2380 Ellsworth Street, Suite D
Berkeley, CA 94704

Colorado Native Plant Society
Box 200
Fort Collins, CO 80522

Florida Native Plant Society
1203 Orange Avenue
Winter Park, FL 32789

Georgia Botanical Society
c/o Marie B. Mellinger
Route 1
Tiger, GA 30576

Idaho Native Plant Society
Pahove Chapter
Box 9451
Boise, ID 83707

Michigan Botanical Club
c/o Dr. John Beaman
Department of Botany and Plant Pathology
Michigan State University
East Lansing, MI 48824

Missouri Native Plant Society
c/o Dr. Jim Wilson
Missouri Department of Conservation
Box 180
Jefferson City, MO 65102

Native Plant Society of New Mexico
Box 5917
Los Lunas, NM 87501

New England Wildflower Society
Garden in the Woods
Hemenway Road
Framingham, MA 01701

North Carolina Wildflower Preservation Society
c/o North Carolina Botanical Garden
UNC-CH Totten Center, 457-A
Chapel Hill, NC 27514

Northern Nevada Native Plant Society
Box 8965
Reno, NV 89507

Oklahoma Native Plant Society
c/o Drs. Connie and John Taylor
Route 1, Box 157
Durant, OK 74701

Native Plant Society of Oregon
c/o David Wagner
Department of Biology
University of Oregon
Eugene, OR 97403

Tennessee Native Plant Society
Department of Botany
University of Tennessee
Knoxville, TN 37916

Texas Native Plant Society
c/o Green Horizons
500 Thompson Drive
Kerrville, TX 78028

Utah Native Plant Society
The State Arboretum of Utah
University of Utah
Salt Lake City, UT 84112

Virginia Wildflower
Preservation Society
Box 844
Annandale, VA 22003

Washington Native Plant Society
c/o Arthur R. Kruckebery
Department of Botany
University of Washington
Seattle, WA 98195

Wyoming Native Plant Society
1603 Capitol Avenue
Cheyenne, WY 82001

*Cornus canadensis **is a 6-inch perennial groundcover form of dogwood. It is a native of the Northwest coast, to Alaska and eastward.***

INDEX

INDEX OF PLANTS

U.S. MEASURE AND METRIC MEASURE CONVERSION CHART

Formulas for Exact Measures | **Rounded Measures for Quick Reference**

	Symbol	When you know:	Multiply by	To find:			
Mass (Weight)	oz	ounces	28.35	grams	1 oz		= 30 g
	lb	pounds	0.45	kilograms	4 oz		= 115 g
	g	grams	0.035	ounces	8 oz		= 225 g
	kg	kilograms	2.2	pounds	16 oz	= 1 lb	= 450 kg
					32 oz	= 2 lb	= 900 kg
					36 oz	= 2 1/4 lb	= 1000g (a kg)
Volume	tsp	teaspoons	5.0	milliliters	1/4 tsp	= 1/24 oz	= 1 ml
	tbsp	tablespoons	15.0	milliliters	1/2 tsp	= 1/12 oz	= 2 ml
	fl oz	fluid ounces	29.57	milliliters	1 tsp	= 1/6 oz	= 5 ml
	c	cups	0.24	liters	1 tbsp	= 1/2 oz	= 15 ml
	pt	pints	0.47	liters	1 c	= 8 oz	= 250 ml
	qt	quarts	0.95	liters	2 c (1 pt)	= 16 oz	= 500 ml
	gal	gallons	3.785	liters	4 c (1 qt)	= 32 oz	= 1 l
	ml	milliters	0.034	fluid ounces	4 qt (1 gal)	= 128 oz	= 3 3/4- l
Length	in.	inches	2.54	centimeters	3/8 in.	= 1 cm	
	ft	feet	30.48	centimeters	1 in.	= 2.5 cm	
	yd	yards	0.9144	meters	2 in.	= 5 cm	
	mi	miles	1.609	kilometers	2-1/2 in.	= 6.5 cm	
	km	kilometers	0.621	miles	12 in. (1 ft)	= 30 cm	
	m	meters	1.094	yards	1 yd	= 90 cm	
	cm	centimeters	0.39	inches	100 ft	= 30 m	
					1 mi	= 1.6 km	
Temperature	°F	Fahrenheit	5/9 (after subtracting 32)	Celsius	32°F	= 0°C	
	°C	Celsius	9/5 (then add 32)	Fahrenheit	68°F	= 20°C	
					212°F	= 100°C	
Area	in.²	square inches	6.452	square centimeters	1 in.²	= 6.5 cm²	
	ft²	square feet	929.0	square centimeters	1 ft²	= 930 cm²	
	yd²	square yards	8361.0	square centimeters	1 yd²	= 8360 cm²	
	a	acres	0.4047	hectares	1 a	= 4050 m²	